SAS for R Users

SAS for R Users

A Book for Data Scientists

Ajay Ohri

Delhi, IN

Registered Office
John Wiley & Sons, Inc., 111 River Street, Hoboken, NJ 07030, USA

Editorial Office
111 River Street, Hoboken, NJ 07030, USA

For details of our global editorial offices, customer services, and more information about Wiley products visit us at www.wiley.com.

Wiley also publishes its books in a variety of electronic formats and by print-on-demand. Some content that appears in standard print versions of this book may not be available in other formats.

Library of Congress Cataloging-in-Publication Data

Names: Ohri, (Ajay), author.
Title: SAS for R users : a book for data scientists / Ajay Ohri.
Description: First edition. | Hoboken, NJ : John Wiley & Sons, Inc., 2020.
  | Includes bibliographical references and index.
Identifiers: LCCN 2019021408 (print) | ISBN 9781119256410 (pbk.)
Subjects: LCSH: SAS (Computer program language) | R (Computer program
  language) | Statistics–Data processing.
Classification: LCC QA76.73.S27 O44 2020 (print) | LCC QA76.73.S27
  (ebook) | DDC 005.5/5–dc23
LC record available at https://lccn.loc.gov/2019021408
LC ebook record available at https://lccn.loc.gov/2019980765

Cover Design: Wiley
Cover Image: © DmitriyRazinkov/Shutterstock

Set in 10/12pt Warnock by SPi Global, Pondicherry, India

Printed in the United States of America

V10012711_080519

This book is dedicated to my students and my family, my son Kush Ohri, members of my church, and my God Jesus Christ.

Contents

Preface

I would like to thank the generosity of the SAS Institute and its employees to provide SAS On Demand for Academics for free without whom this book would not exist. In addition, I also want to thank the baristas from Starbucks Gurgaon. These are the people who downvote my questions on Stackoverflow. You inspire me guys.

SAS for R users is aimed at entry-level data scientists. It is not aimed at researchers in academia nor is it aimed at high- end data scientists working on Big Data, deep learning, or machine learning. In short, it is merely aimed at human learning business analytics (or data science as it is now called).

Both SAS and R are widely used languages and yet both are very different. SAS is a programming language that was designed in the 1960s which is broadly divided into Data Steps and a wide variety of Procedure or PROC steps, while R is an object oriented, mostly functional, language designed in the 1990s.

There are many, many books covering either but only very few books covering both.

Why then write the book? After all, I have written two books on R, and one on Python for R. SAS language remains the most widely used language in enterprises, contributing directly to the brand name, and profitability of one of the largest private software companies that invests hugely in its own research instead of borrowing research in the name of open source. A statistics student knowing Python (esp Machine Learning ML), R, SAS, Big Data (esp Spark ML), Data Visualization (using Tableau) is a mythical unicorn unavailable to recruiters who often have to settle for a few of these skills and then train them in house.

As a teacher, I want my students to have jobs – there is no ideological tilt to open source or any company here. The probability of students getting jobs from campus greatly increases if they know BOTH SAS and R not just one of them. That is why this book has been written.

Scope

This book is designed for professionals and students; people who want to enter data science and who have a coding background with some basics of statistical information. It is not aimed at researchers or people who like giraffes and do not read the book from the beginning.

1

About SAS and R

Here is a brief introduction about R and SAS,instructions about installations and a broad high-level comparison.

1.1   About SAS

SAS used to be called the Statistical Analysis System Software suite developed by the SAS Institute for advanced analytics, business intelligence, data management, and predictive analytics. Developed at North Carolina State University from 1966 until 1976, when the SAS Institute was incorporated. It was then further developed in the 1980s and 1990s with the additional statistical procedures and components. SAS is a language, a software suite and a company created by Anthony James Barr and James Goodnight along with two others. For purposes of this book we will use SAS for SAS computer language.

- SAS also provides a graphical point and click user interface for non-technical users.

While a graduate student in statistics at North Carolina State University, James Goodnight wrote a computer program for analyzing agricultural data. After a few years, James's application had attracted a diverse and loyal following among its users, and the program's data management and reporting capabilities had expanded beyond James's original intentions.

In 1976, he decided to work at developing and marketing his product on a full-time basis, and the SAS Institute was founded. Since its beginning, a distinguishing feature of the company has been its attentiveness to users of the software. Today, the SAS Institute is the world's largest privately-held software company, and Dr. James Goodnight is its CEO. He continues to be actively involved as a developer of SAS System software as well as being one of the most widely respected CEOs in the community.

SAS for R Users: A Book for Data Scientists, First Edition. Ajay Ohri.
© 2020 John Wiley & Sons, Inc. Published 2020 by John Wiley & Sons, Inc.

The SAS System has more than 200 components

- Base SAS – Basic procedures and data management
- SAS/STAT – Statistical analysis
- SAS/GRAPH – Graphics and presentation
- SAS/OR – Operations research
- SAS/ETS – Econometrics and Time Series Analysis
- SAS/IML – Interactive matrix language

The SAS University Edition includes the SAS products Base SAS®, SAS/STAT®, SAS/IML®, SAS/ACCESS® Interface to PC Files, and SAS Studio. SAS has an annual license fee and almost 98% return to SAS every year, voting by their chequebook. All these products are Copyright © SAS Institute Inc., SAS Campus Drive, Cary, North Carolina 27513, USA. (https://decisionstats.com/2009/08/20/the-top-decisionstats-articles-part-1-analytics/and https://en.wikipedia.org/wiki/SAS_(software))

1.1.1 Installation

While SAS Software for Enterprises is priced at an annual license, for students, researchers and learners you can choose from the SAS University Edition (a virtual machine) at https://www.sas.com/en_in/software/university-edition.html or SAS on Demand at https://odamid.oda.sas.com/SASLogon/login (a software as a service running SAS in browser).

To install the SAS University Edition on your Virtual machine you can follow the following steps (I am using VMware Workstation for this):

- Run your Virtual Machine and click on file.
- Open and select SAS University Edition (the extension of the file should be .ova). You can provide a new name and storage path for your new Virtual Machine and then import.
- Now, you need to initially run the virtual machine and use the link provided in the VM to connect to the SAS University Edition in your browser.

1.2 About R

R is a language and environment for statistical computing and graphics. It is a **GNU project** which is similar to the S language and environment which was developed at Bell Laboratories (formerly AT&T, now Lucent Technologies) by John Chambers and colleagues. R can be considered as a different implementation of S. R was initially written by Robert Gentleman and Ross Ihaka.

1.2.1   The R Environment

From https://www.r-project.org/about.html, R is an integrated suite of software facilities for data manipulation, calculation and graphical display. It includes:

- an effective data handling and storage facility,
- a suite of operators for calculations on arrays, in particular matrices,
- a large, coherent, integrated collection of intermediate tools for data analysis,
- graphical facilities for data analysis and display either on-screen or on hardcopy, and
- a well-developed, simple and effective programming language which includes conditionals, loops, user-defined recursive functions and input and output facilities.

There are almost 14 000+ packages in R (https://www.rdocumentation.org). You can also look at specific views of packages (https://cran.r-project.org/web/views is a task view like a bundle or cluster of packages with similar usage i.e. econometrics). For computationally-intensive tasks, C, C++ and Fortran code can be linked and called at run time. Advanced users can write C code to manipulate R objects directly.

1.2.2   Installation of R

You can download and install R from https://www.r-project.org (or specifically from https://cloud.r-project.org for your operating system). You can then download and install the IDE RStudio from https://www.rstudio.com/products/rstudio/download/#download. Lastly, you can install any of 12 000+ packages (see https://cran.r-project.org/web/views and https://www.rdocumentation.org) using **install.packages("PACKAGENAME")** from within R. These packages can be downloaded from the CRAN (Comprehensive R Archive Network).

Within https://www.datacamp.com/community/tutorials/r-packages-guide, R packages are collections of functions and datasets developed by the community. They increase the power of R either by improving existing base R functionalities, or by adding new ones. For example, you can use sqldf package to use SQL with R and RODBC package to connect to RDBMS databases.

In addition, an excellent resource is how to learn SAS for R users from the SAS Institute itself.

https://support.sas.com/edu/schedules.html?ctry=us&crs=SP4R

The e-learning course is free as of October 2018. The course teaches the following:

- how to read and write SAS programs
- import various forms of data
- subset and merge data tables including using SQL (by the Proc SQL procedure)
- carry out iterative processing and simulate new data
- create new variables and functions
- create and enhance plots of all types
- apply descriptive and inferential procedures, including regression, logistic regression, analysis of variance, stepwise model selection, and mixed models
- conduct matrix algebra and statistical simulations in the interactive matrix language (IML)
- call R from SAS to use as a complimentary resource.

1.3 Notable Points in SAS and R Languages

1) Each line in SAS ends with; R does not have any such limitation
2) SAS is case insensitive – ozone and OZone are the same thing. R is case sensitive.
3) In SAS comments are within /* */ (press Ctrl + /). In R comments follow #
4) SAS has two kinds of statements:
   a) Data Step which deals with input, manipulation of data and

```
data ajay;
set input;
run;
```

   b) Proc Step which are procedural steps for analysis and output.

```
proc contents data = ajay;
run;
```

R has functions and packages for similar functions bundled together
5) SAS needs a license for extra functionality (e.g., for Time Series you needed SAS /ETS license) while R is free and extensible (forecast package for Time Series).

1.4 Some Important Functions with Comparative Comparisons Respectively

A Proc by Proc comparison in SAS language with R language functions is shown below. It will be explained in greater detail in later chapters. Some people consider R's smaller syntax helpful in coding while others consider SAS to be easier to learn and focus on analysis instead.

Function	SAS	R
Import data Print data	proc import proc print data=ajay; run;	read_csv (readr package) ajay
Structure of Data Object	proc contents data=ajay; run;	str(ajay)
Frequency of Categorical Variables (Cross Tabulation)	proc freq data= ajay; tables var1*var2; run;	table(ajay$var1,ajay$var2)
Analysis of Numerical Variables without/ with grouped by another variable	Proc means Proc means data= ajay; Var var1 var2; Run; Proc means daya=ajay; Var var1 var2; Class grp1; run;	summary(ajay$var1,ajay$var2) library(Hmisc) summarize(ajay$var1,ajay$grp 1,summary) summarize(ajay$var1,ajay$grp 1,summary)

1.5 Summary

In this chapter we have introduced R and SAS languages, and briefly compared their main functions/syntax.

1.6 Quiz Questions

1 Who is the CEO of SAS?

2 When was SAS founded?

3 Where was SAS founded?

4 Who designed R?

5 When was R founded?

6 Where was R founded?

7 Which of the two languages has a better documentation and customer support?

8 TASK: Suppose you know SQL. Can you identify functions or packages you can use in SAS and R respectively to run SQL commands?

Quiz Answers

1 JAMES GOODNIGHT

2 1976

3 NORTH CAROLINA STATE UNIVERSITY

4 ROSS IHAKA AND ROBERT GENTLEMAN

5 1993

6 UNIVERSITY OF AUCKLAND

7 SAS

8 IN SAS: use proc. sql, IN R: use sqldf package.

2

Data Input, Import and Print

2.1 Importing Data

Importing data is the first step in analyzing data. It is important that you have reliable and relevant data. You should be able to import data correctly because the computer processes what data you input. If the imported data is faulty, the analysis that you will receive after performing various tasks on it will also be erroneous and misleading.

This concept is also commonly known as GIGO (Garbage In Garbage OUT). Therefore, the input step is one of the most important steps in the data science pipeline. There could also be different ways to input data in R and SAS from files or from data connections. Importing of datasets calls for certain functions in R whereas it calls for certain procedures for the same in SAS.

2.1.1 Packages in R

Importing of data in R can be done using certain packages and functions, and to use those packages, we need to install them in our application.

Installing a package has the following command in R:

```
install.packages("package_name")
```

After installation to use this package you must load that package. Loading a package means getting the package in active state (session). To load a package use:

```
library("package_name")
```

Updating a package:

```
update.packages("package_name")
```

Note that we install the package only once, we update it occasionally and we load it every time we begin a R session. To unload a package, we use:

```
detach.packages("package_name")
```

To uninstall a package we use:

```
uninstall.packages("package_name")
```

2.2 Importing Data in SAS

Here we study multiple ways to input data.

In SAS to save space you can put this in the beginning options compress = yes;

2.2.1 Data Input in SAS

Data Input in SAS manually has been an easy task, and there are a certain set of examples where you can easily learn how to input data in SAS.

The INPUT statement reads raw data from instream data lines or external files into a SAS dataset. Data input is the first step for every analysis, without any dataset or data there can be no analysis of any kind. Data input can be done in various forms. Let's look at a few examples of data input in SAS.

In the examples given below, we have input normal numerical data, strings, names etc.

```
data first;
infile datalines
input m n;
datalines;
5 10
10 20
20 40
;
run;
```

The code above creates a dataset named first.

- infile statement is used to specify the type of data to be read.
- input statement is used to specify the names, number and type of variables being read.
- datalines statement is used to specify that the following lines contain the data to be read.
- The keyword "cards" can also be used instead of "datalines."

```
data second;
infile datalines
input name$ points;
datalines;
ajay 10
kush 9
;
run;
```

```
data third;
infile datalines missover dsd;
input m n o;
,2,3
4,,6
7,8,9
```

- $ sign is used to specify that the variable it follows is a character variable
- Missover option is used to prevent the data step from going to the next line if it does not find values for all variables in the input statement in the current record.
- dsd option is used to treat commas as separator characters.

Code to import in SAS is different from R because in R we use functions whereas in SAS we generally call procedures. R is an object-oriented language.

Using the Import Wizard is an easy and straightforward way to import existing data with well-behaved formatting into SAS. There are other methods for importing data into SAS like proc. import, or even entering raw observations into SAS itself to create a new dataset.

These methods of importing or creating data can give you greater control over how to read variables (the informats), how to write the variables (the formats), how to parse the data (delimited, aligned, repetition, etc.), and more.

2.2.2 Using Proc Import to Import a Raw File

```
proc import out=dataset_name
DBMS= file_type
datafile= 'file_path';
getnames=yes;
run;
```

Here we use the proc. import step to import a raw data file and save it as an SAS dataset. DBMS is used to specify the file type, e.g.: CSV, XLS etc.

getnames = *yes* is to specify that the first row contains column names.

Note: The type of dataset created (temporary or permanent) depends on the name you specify in the out = statement.

A permanent dataset has to be referenced by a two-level name: - **library_name**.*data_set_name* whereas a temporary dataset just has a one-level name.

2.2.3 Creating a temporary dataset from a permanent one using "set"

```
data temp_setname;
  set libname.permaset_name;
  run;
```

2.3 Importing Data in R

There are a number of ways to import data into R, and several formats are available:

1) From CSV files using readr or data. Table package
2) From Excel to R
3) From SAS to R
4) From SPSS to R
5) From Stata to R, and more
6) From Relational Databases (RDBMS) using RODBC
7) From json files using jsonlite package

https://rforanalytics.wordpress.com/useful-links-for-r/odbc-databases-for-r

Let us explore some of the ways to import data in R.

2.3.1 Importing from Comma Separated Value (CSV) Files

There are three functions which can be used to import csv files in R:

1) read.csv() or read. Table() which are in the utils package which is installed and loaded by default.

```
read.csv("file_path.csv") or read.table("file_path.csv")
```

2) read_csv which is in the readr package.

```
install.packages("readr")
          library("readr")


                    read_csv("file_path.csv")
```

3) fread() which is in the data. Table package.

```
install.packages("data.table")
          library("data.table")


                    fread("file_path.csv")
```

```
fread and read_csv  are the fastest of all these.
```

You can use the system. Time() function to verify that as follows:

```
system.time(read.csv("file_path.csv"))
system.time(read_csv("file_path.csv"))

system.time(fread("file_path.csv"))
```

2.3.2 Importing from Excel Files

We need to install readxl package and use the read_excel function to import .xls or .xlsx types of files.

```
install.packages("readxl")
library("readxl")

read_excel("file_path.xls")
```

Example: To import sheet 1 of an excel file with the first row as column names

```
read_excel("MySpreadSheet.xls", sheet=1, col_names=TRUE)
```

We can also use sheet names put within double quotes instead of the sheet number to specify the sheet we want from any excel file.

2.3.3 Importing from SAS

read.sas7bdat() from sas7bdat package is used to import .sas7bdat files

```
install.packages("sas7bdat")
library("sas7bdat")
read.sas7bdat("file_path.sas7bdat")
```

2.3.4 Importing from SPSS and STATA

We use the read.spss () and read.dta() function from foreign package to import SPSS and STATA files respectively.

```
install.packages("foreign")
library("foreign")
read.spss("file_path.spss")
read.dta("file_path.dta")
```

2.3.5 Assigning the Values Imported to a Data Object in R

Assigning in R has the following syntax:

```
objectname=value;
or
objectname <- value;
```

The following code is used to assign the imported file to an object.

```
objectname=read_csv("file_path",parameters)
```

Similarly, data read using other functions can be assigned to R objects.

Note: Each of the functions used to import data discussed above take in more parameters which define certain formatting to be done on the data while importing.

To manually input we use the following

```
> ajay=c(11,2,30)
> ajay
[1] 11 2 30
```

We can do the same for other types of data except string variables which will be in quotes (i.e. "ten")

2.4   Providing Data Input

We can also create datasets, vectors or matrices by using the input value given by us.

2.4.1   Data Input in R

2.4.1.1   Using the c() function is the simplest way to create a list in R

We can input numerical, dates and string values as follows:

```
ajay=c(10,20,30,40)
dates2=c("26jun98","1/09/2005","1January2016")
newone=c("Raj","Shiva","Kamal","Ajay")
```

2.4.1.2   Providing missing values to the vector

NA in R signifies missing values (in SAS a missing value is denoted by a single period.)

```
ajay2=c(23,45,78,NA,NA,89,NA)
```

```
is.na(ajay2)
## [1] FALSE FALSE FALSE  TRUE  TRUE FALSE  TRUE
```

is.na() function is used to detect missing values in the vector.

2.4.1.3   To Input multiple columns of data

```
ajay3=data.frame(c("a","b"),c(1,2))
```

This creates a data frame with two columns as follows:

```
a 1
b 2
```

or, we can create a matrix using:

```
my_matrix = matrix(
  c(2, 4, 3, 1, 5, 7),
   nrow=3,
   ncol=2)
```

This code makes a matrix with values in c() arranged in three rows and two columns arranged column wise. Note: vector and matrix must have all values of the same type but data frames can have values of different types.

2.4.1.4   Using loops to input

```
ajay=NULL
for (i in 1:20) {
  ajay[i]=i}
print(ajay)

Output

1 2 3 4 5 6 7 8 9 10 11 12 13 14 15 16 17 18 19 20
```

2.5   Data Input in SAS

Data Input in SAS manually has been an easy task, however, there are a certain set of examples where you can easily learn how to input data in SAS.

The INPUT statement reads raw data from instream data lines or external files into an SAS dataset. Data input is the first step for every analysis; without any dataset or data there can be no analysis of any kind. Data input could be done in various forms lets see few examples of data input in SAS.

In the examples given below, we have input normal numerical data, strings, names etc.

```
data first;
infile datalines
input m n;
datalines;
5 10
10 20
20 40
;
run;
```

This code creates a dataset named first.

infile statement is used to specify the type of data to be read.
input statement is used to specify the names, number and type of variables
    being read.
datalines statement is used to specify that the following lines contain the data
    to be read.
The keyword "cards" can also be used instead of "datalines."

```
data second;
infile datalines ;
input name$ points;
datalines;
ajay 10
kush 9
;
run;
```

$ sign is used to specify that the variable it follows is a character variable

```
data third;
infile datalines missover dsd;
input m n o;
datalines;
,2,3
4,,6
7,8,9
;
run;
```

Missover option is used to prevent the data step from going to the next line
if it does not find values for all variables in the input statement in the current
record. Here the dsd option is used to treat commas as separator characters.

2.6   Printing Data

After importing the data, the next important step is to print that data to have a look at the type of data you now have to analyze.

2.6.1   Print in SAS

Printing the dataset in SAS involves calling the print procedure in SAS. The code below will help you print the whole dataset named ajaydat.

```
proc print data=ajaydat;

run;
```

The code below will help you print the first five observations of the dataset named ajaydat.

```
proc print data=ajaydat(obs=5);

run;
```

The code below will help you print the observations ranging from 10 to 20 for dataset ajaydat.

```
proc print data=ajaydat(firstobs=10 obs=20)

run;
```

2.6.2   Print in R

In R, printing of data does not need any function or package. You simply write the dataset name and then run it to print the data.

If you read data in mydata and write the data_set name:

The whole data in mydata will be printed at console.

```
mydata=read_csv("file_path")
        mydata
```

Only the first observation of mydata is printed to the console. Default value of n is 6.

```
head(mydata,n)
```

Observations ranging from 10 to 20 would be displayed.

```
mydata[10:20]
```

2.7   Summary

Importing data in R requires a variety of functions to import different types of files whereas proc. import is used with different options or parameters to import any type of file in SAS. Data input in R is done using the c() function and using a data step with input option in SAS. In R, printing a dataset just requires the writing of the name of the dataset and running it, whereas SAS uses proc. print to print any dataset.

2.8   Quiz Questions

1   How will you load an installed package in R?

2   Give three functions which can be used to import csv files in R.

3   Which package contains read_csv() and fread() respectively?

4   Which function in R can you use to measure the time taken by a code to execute?

5   Which procedure in SAS is used to import raw data files?

6   How can you create a temporary dataset from a permanent one in SAS using a data step?

7   Which wildcard is used to specify that a particular variable is a character variable in SAS?

8   What is the missover option used for in the infile statement in a SAS data step?

9 How will you print a data set in R?

10 Which procedure is used to print a data set in SAS?

Quiz Answers

1 library("package_name")

2 read_csv(),fread(),read.csv()

3 readr, data.table

4 system.time()

5 proc. import

6
```
data temp_setname; set libname.permaset_name; run;
```

7 $

8 Missover tells SAS not to jump to the next line if it does not find values for all variables. We just type the name of the dataset and run it to print a data set in R.

9 Just type the name of object

10 proc print

3

Data Inspection and Cleaning

3.1 Introduction

Data Cleaning and Inspection is the next important part of the data analysis pipeline. It implies that before starting analysis, visualization or machine learning and its insights, you should have cleaned any data that has to be analyzed. Though Machine Learning, Exploratory Data Analysis and Data Visualization take up more time in analytical education, in an actual data science project much more time is spent in data inspection and cleaning.

3.2 Data Inspection

Data inspection helps us determine that data import has been executed correctly, that variables are in same length (rows) and breadth (columns) and that variables (columns) are in the same format as expected.

3.2.1 Data Inspection in SAS

Let's try this in SAS

- Referring to a column is easier in SAS than in R

```
/* Refer to a column by using var in proc and keeping it by keep in data step*/
data import4 (keep=ozone2);
set import3;
run;
```

Creating a new variable which is twice the size of target column

```
data import4;
set import4;
ozone3=2*ozone2;
run;
```

SAS for R Users: A Book for Data Scientists, First Edition. Ajay Ohri.
© 2020 John Wiley & Sons, Inc. Published 2020 by John Wiley & Sons, Inc.

Printing only that variable by using var (which is also used in other Procs)

```
proc print data=import3 (obs=5);
var ozone2;
run;
```

- Referring to a row is more complex in SAS than R

```
proc print data=import3 (obs=7);
run;
```

Obs	Wind	Temp	Month	Day	Ozone2	Solar_R2	var2
1	7.4	67	5	1	41.0000	190.000	.
2	8	72	5	2	36.0000	118.000	.
3	12.6	74	5	3	12.0000	149.000	.
4	11.5	62	5	4	18.0000	313.000	.
5	14.3	56	5	5	35.3017	185.932	.
6	14.9	66	5	6	28.0000	185.932	.
7	8.6	65	5	7	23.0000	299.000	.

Using a do loop for getting certain rows

```
data output1;
   do i = 1, 3, 4, 7;
      set import3 point = i;
      output;
   end;
   stop;
run;

proc print data=output1;
run;
```

Obs	Wind	Temp	Month	Day	Ozone2	Solar_R2	var2
1	7.4	67	5	1	41	190	.
2	12.6	74	5	3	12	149	.
3	11.5	62	5	4	18	313	.
4	8.6	65	5	7	23	299	.

3.2.2 Data Inspection in R

- head gives first 6 values
- names give names of columns
- dim gives dimensions (row column)
- str gives structure (type of variables, variable names, dimensions) type of data object
- class gives type of data object (which is important in R as it can be many different types of object)
- summary gives a summary of the whole object including numerical analysis, presence of missing values and frequencies of factor variables.

```
> data(airquality)
> head(airquality)
  Ozone Solar.R Wind Temp Month Day
1    41     190  7.4   67     5   1
2    36     118  8.0   72     5   2
3    12     149 12.6   74     5   3
4    18     313 11.5   62     5   4
5    NA      NA 14.3   56     5   5
6    28      NA 14.9   66     5   6
> names(airquality)
[1] "Ozone"   "Solar.R" "Wind"    "Temp"    "Month"   "Day"
> dim(airquality)
[1] 153 6
> str(airquality)
'data.frame':  153 obs. of  6 variables:
 $ Ozone  : int  41 36 12 18 NA 28 23 19 8 NA ...
 $ Solar.R: int  190 118 149 313 NA NA 299 99 19 194 ...
 $ Wind   : num  7.4 8 12.6 11.5 14.3 14.9 8.6 13.8 20.1 8.6 ...
 $ Temp   : int  67 72 74 62 56 66 65 59 61 69 ...
 $ Month  : int  5 5 5 5 5 5 5 5 5 5 ...
 $ Day    : int  1 2 3 4 5 6 7 8 9 10 ...
>class(airquality)
[1] "data.frame"
> summary(airquality)
     Ozone           Solar.R           Wind             Temp           Month             Day
 Min.   :  1.00   Min.   :  7.0   Min.   : 1.700   Min.   :56.00   Min.   :5.000   Min.   : 1.0
 1st Qu.: 18.00   1st Qu.:115.8   1st Qu.: 7.400   1st Qu.:72.00   1st Qu.:6.000   1st Qu.: 8.0
 Median : 31.50   Median :205.0   Median : 9.700   Median :79.00   Median :7.000   Median :16.0
 Mean   : 42.13   Mean   :185.9   Mean   : 9.958   Mean   :77.88   Mean   :6.993   Mean   :15.8
 3rd Qu.: 63.25   3rd Qu.:258.8   3rd Qu.:11.500   3rd Qu.:85.00   3rd Qu.:8.000   3rd Qu.:23.0
 Max.   :168.00   Max.   :334.0   Max.   :20.700   Max.   :97.00   Max.   :9.000   Max.   :31.0
 NA's   :37       NA's   :7
> class(airquality)
[1] "data.frame"
```

We can choose specific parts of a data frame by using square brackets, i.e.

- airquality [2,3] gives data in second row and third column of airquality
- airquality [2,] gives data in second row and all columns of airquality
- airquality [,3] gives data in all rows and third column of airquality
- airquality [R,C] gives data in Rth row and Cth column of airquality

airquality$Ozone gives value of Ozone column in airquality

3.3 Missing Values

Data that is missing can be due to human data input error, formatting issues or incorrect coding syntax for import. It is a problem because we cannot have analysis without data.

There are three ways to handle missing data:

1) Ignore it
2) Delete it
3) Replace it – Replace with a value that does not change the numerical properties significantly. Missing value imputation is the name given to replacing missing data. At its simplest form we replace missing values by either mean or median data. At its more sophisticated form, we use correlation from other variables that are more complete to impute them. We can also use machine learning algorithms to impute data from other variables. Specific packages like mice package in R help with more sophisticated missing value imputation.

3.3.1 Missing Values in SAS

File Import

```
FILENAME REFFILE '/home/ajay4/book/airquality.csv';

PROC IMPORT DATAFILE=REFFILE
     DBMS=CSV
     OUT=WORK.IMPORT;
     GETNAMES=YES;
RUN;
```

Finding variable type. To our surprise many variables have been encoded as string variables in SAS which were encoded as numeric in R. This is due to NA being a character value in SAS but missing values in R. In SAS missing values are denoted by a single period.

```
PROC CONTENTS DATA=WORK.IMPORT; RUN;

Alphabetic List of Variables and Attributes
#    Variable    Type    Len    Format    Informat
7    Day         Num     8      BEST12.   BEST32.
6    Month       Num     8      BEST12.   BEST32.
2    Ozone       Char    2      $2.       $2.
3    Solar.R     Char    3      $3.       $3.
5    Temp        Num     8      BEST12.   BEST32.
1    VAR1        Char    4      $4.       $4.
4    Wind        Num     8      BEST12.   BEST32.
```

Let's print the first six rows of data (similar to head function in R)

```
proc print data =import (obs=6);
run;

Obs   VAR1   Ozone   Solar.R   Wind   Temp   Month   Day
1     1      41      190       7.4    67     5       1
2     2      36      118       8      72     5       2
3     3      12      149       12.6   74     5       3
4     4      18      313       11.5   62     5       4
5     5      NA      NA        14.3   56     5       5
6     6      28      NA        14.9   66     5       6
```

Let's replace NA in SAS

If we had to replace NA in just one variable, we can use compress

```
data import2;
set import;
Ozone=compress(Ozone,"NA","");
Run;

proc contents data=import2;
run;
```

However, if we wanted to replace it in all character variables, we use an SAS function called array with a 'for' loop and an 'if' statement. We convert character variable one by one into numeric variables and drop the original. A point to note is to avoid a dot in variable names in SAS. Drop is used in SAS to drop a certain variable in the SAS dataset.

```
data import2;
 set import;

 array Chars[*] _character_;
 do i = 1 to dim(Chars);

     Chars[i] = strip(Chars[i]);
  if  Chars[i] = "NA" then Chars[i] =. ;
 end;
 drop i;
```

```
Ozone2=input(Ozone,2.);
drop Ozone ;

Solar_R2=input(SolarR,3.);
drop SolarR ;
var2=input(VAR1,8.);
drop VAR1 ;
run;

proc means data=import2 n nmiss mean;
run;
```

Using nmiss we can find and ignore the missing values in proc means (similar to na.rm. = T in R)

The MEANS Procedure

Variable	N	N Miss	Mean
Wind	153	0	9.9575163
Temp	153	0	77.8823529
Month	153	0	6.9934641
Day	153	0	15.8039216
Ozone2	116	37	35.3017241
Solar_R2	146	7	185.9315068
var2	0	153	

Suppose we ran the same Proc Means procedure but without nmiss, we will not see the missing values (is.na = T in R).

The MEANS Procedure

Variable	Mean
Wind	9.9575163
Temp	77.8823529
Month	6.9934641
Day	15.8039216
Ozone2	35.3017241
Solar_R2	185.9315068
var2	

But for character variables and others there is the following representation:

Missing Values	Representation in Data
Numeric	. (a single point)
Character	' ' (a blank enclosed in quotes)

For replacing a missing value in a character variable you can use:

```
if var=' ' then do;
```

To simply omit all missing values (like na.omit in R) we use the following SAS code:

```
data import21;
set import2;
if Ozone2=. then delete;
run;

proc means data=import21 n nmiss mean;
Run;
```

You can see a few rows that also had solar_R2 have been deleted. Therefore, we need to be careful about explicit deletion.

The MEANS Procedure

Variable	N	N Miss	Mean
Wind	116	0	9.8620690
Temp	116	0	77.8706897
Month	116	0	7.1982759
Day	116	0	15.5344828
Ozone2	116	0	35.3017241
Solar_R2	111	5	184.8018018
var2	0	116	

To **replace missing values with the mean of the variable** you can use the following:

```
proc stdize data=import2 reponly method=mean out=import3;
var ozone2 solar_r2;
Run;

proc print data=import2 (obs=6);
var ozone2 solar_r2;
run;
Obs      Ozone2       Solar_R2
1         41           190
2         36           118
3         12           149
4         18           313
5          .            .
6         28            .
proc print data=import3 (obs=6);
var ozone2 solar_r2;
run;

Obs      Ozone2       Solar_R2
1        41.0000      190.000
2        36.0000      118.000
3        12.0000      149.000
4        18.0000      313.000
5        35.3017      185.932
6        28.0000      185.932
```

3.3.2 Missing Values in R

Let's do this in R

```
> data(airquality)
> summary(airquality)
     Ozone          Solar.R          Wind            Temp           Month            Day
 Min.   :  1.00   Min.   :  7.0   Min.   : 1.700   Min.   :56.00   Min.   :5.000   Min.   : 1.0
 1st Qu.: 18.00   1st Qu.:115.8   1st Qu.: 7.400   1st Qu.:72.00   1st Qu.:6.000   1st Qu.: 8.0
 Median : 31.50   Median :205.0   Median : 9.700   Median :79.00   Median :7.000   Median :16.0
 Mean   : 42.13   Mean   :185.9   Mean   : 9.958   Mean   :77.88   Mean   :6.993   Mean   :15.8
 3rd Qu.: 63.25   3rd Qu.:258.8   3rd Qu.:11.500   3rd Qu.:85.00   3rd Qu.:8.000   3rd Qu.:23.0
 Max.   :168.00   Max.   :334.0   Max.   :20.700   Max.   :97.00   Max.   :9.000   Max.   :31.0
 NA's   :37       NA's   :7
```

We see the mean and then check for mean with missing values ignored using na.rm. = T. We also check for total missing values by is.na. In R, as we have mentioned, missing values are given by NA

```
> mean(airquality$Ozone)
[1] NA

Using na.rm+T we ignore missing values (in R they are NA in SAS
  they are . )
> mean(airquality$Ozone,na.rm=T)
[1] 42.12931

> table(is.na(airquality))
FALSE TRUE
 874  44
```

We can delete all missing values by na.omit

```
> airquality2=na.omit(airquality)

> str(airquality)
'data.frame': 153 obs. of 6 variables:
 $ Ozone   : int 41 36 12 18 NA 28 23 19 8 NA ...
 $ Solar.R : int 190 118 149 313 NA NA 299 99 19 194 ...
 $ Wind    : num 7.4 8 12.6 11.5 14.3 14.9 8.6 13.8 20.1 8.6 ...
 $ Temp    : int 67 72 74 62 56 66 65 59 61 69 ...
 $ Month   : int 5 5 5 5 5 5 5 5 5 5 ...
 $ Day     : int 1 2 3 4 5 6 7 8 9 10 ...

> str(airquality2)
'data.frame': 111 obs. of 6 variables:
 $ Ozone   : int 41 36 12 18 23 19 8 16 11 14 ...
 $ Solar.R : int 190 118 149 313 299 99 19 256 290 274 ...
 $ Wind    : num 7.4 8 12.6 11.5 8.6 13.8 20.1 9.7 9.2 10.9 ...
 $ Temp    : int 67 72 74 62 65 59 61 69 66 68 ...
 $ Month   : int 5 5 5 5 5 5 5 5 5 5 ...
 $ Day     : int 1 2 3 4 7 8 9 12 13 14 ...
 - attr(*, "na.action") = 'omit' Named int 5 6 10 11 25 26 27
   32 33 34 ...
 ..- attr(*, "names") = chr "5" "6" "10" "11" ...
```

We can use a conditional operator to replace missing values by median. In the ifelse operator, the first part is condition, the second part is if condition is true and the third part is if condition is false. We put the condition as is.na (which checks for missing value). If is.na is true, it indicates data is missing value then we replace it by median of variable (ignoring missing values) and if is.na is false we do not replace data but keep the original value. This is similar to proc stdize

```
> data("airquality")
> summary(airquality$Ozone)

 Min.   1st Qu. Median   Mean   3rd Qu.  Max.    NA's
 1.00   18.00   31.50    42.13  63.25    168.00  37

> airquality$Ozone=ifelse(is.na(airquality$Ozone),
median(airquality$Ozone,na.rm = T),airquality$Ozone)

> summary(airquality$Ozone)
 Min.   1st Qu.  Median   Mean   3rd Qu.  Max.
 1.00   21.00    31.50    39.56  46.00    168.00
```

3.4   Data Cleaning

Here we try and clean various types of errors in a data type in both SAS and R.

3.4.1   Data Cleaning in SAS

We have input the data in our first step to clean the Data. SAS code to omit this type of errors and create a useful dataset for the purposes of analysis.

We first input data using the SAS datalines way (corresponds to R's c operator for a list).

```
data money;
infile datalines ;
input name$ ;
datalines;
'50000'
'50,000'
'$50000'
50000
'50000'
'50000.00'
;

run;
```

We check if data was input correctly using proc print

```
proc print data=money;
run;
```

Note /* test*/ shows a comment in SAS just like #test shows a comment in R

```
/* Obs      name */
/* 1       '50000' */
/* 2       '50,000' */
/* 3       '$50000' */
/* 4       50000 */
/* 5       '50000.0 */
```

Here we use the **compress** function to get rid of junk values, $ '(just like **gsub** in R).

We also use the **input** function to convert character to numeric value just as we did **as.numeric** function in R.

However, in SAS we have to specify format and informats to convert data types from one to another. In R, we use lubridate, stringr package, and the as operator to do so.

```
data money2;
set money;
name2=compress(name,",$'");
name3 = input(name2,6.);
run;
```

Proc contents is like str in R to check data

```
proc contents data=money2;
run;
```

Proc means is like summary in R (however we can specify only one var by using the var argument in SAS whereas in R we can use the $operator for single variables

```
proc means data=money2;
var name3;
run;
```

```
The output shows our data cleaning was successful.

The MEANS Procedure

Analysis Variable: name3
N    Mean        Std Dev   Minimum     Maximum
6    50 000.00   0         50 000.00   50 000.00
```

3.4.2 Data Cleaning in R

```
> money=c('50000','50,000','$50000',50000,'50000.00')

> mean(money)
[1] NA
Warning message:
In mean.default(money)  : argument is not numeric or logical:
returning NA

> str(money)
 chr [1:5] "50000" "50,000" "$50000" "50000" "50000.00"

> money=gsub(',',",money)
> money
[1] "50000" "50000" "$50000" "50000" "50000.00"

> money=gsub('\\$',",money)
> money
[1] "50000" "50000" "50000" "50000" "50000.00"

> money=as.numeric(money)
> money
[1] 50000 50000 50000 50000 50000

> mean(money)
[1] 50000
> str(money)
 num [1:5] 50000 50000 50000 50000 50000
```

Using the gsub package in R, it is easy to clean Data just as we used compress in SAS. We have created a different variable every time we replace to avoid the actual data to being lost and/or changed. Data cleaning is quite a simple process in both R and SAS thanks to the inbuilt functions as well as documentation. What adds to the complexity is the volume and variety of the data both Big and Small. You can also see data cleaning is an intensive manual task as data errors can be of many types. It is estimated that out of many data science projects as much as 80% of time is spent on data hygiene.

3.5 Quiz Questions

1 How do you represent missing values in SAS?

2 How do you represent missing values in R?

3 How will you replace a missing value by mean in R?

4 How will you replace a missing value by mean in SAS?

5 How will you clean data with junk values like $ and , in R?

6 How will you clean data with junk values like $ and , in SAS?

7 How do you check variable types in SAS?

8 How do you check variable types in R?

9 How do you print only variable in SAS?

10 How do you print only variable in R?

Quiz Answers

1 X.

2 NA.

3 Using ifelse

4 proc stdize

5 gsub

6 compress

7 proc contents

8 str

9 Use var in proc print like

```
proc print data=datasetname;
var variablename;
run;
```

10 Use $ operator like

```
datasetname$variablename
```

4

Handling Dates, Strings, Numbers

So far, we have learnt how to import data and create your own data in R and SAS, along with data inspection and cleaning. Here, we will learn how to work with different kinds of data, for example, dates, strings and numbers and how to convert one data format to another in both R and SAS. This includes handling numeric data, manipulating string/character variables (i.e. by extracting a substring of a string variable), handling different types of date format and numeric calculations with dates (i.e. difference between dates) as well as categorical data.

4.1 Working with Numeric Data

Integral types represent only whole numbers (positive, negative, and zero), and *nonintegral* types represent numbers with both integer and fractional parts.

4.1.1 Handling Numbers in SAS

Assigning Numeric Values to Variables

```
data ajay2;
a="1234567";
Run;

proc print data=ajay2;
Run;
Obs     a
1      1234567
```

We multiply the character variable by 1 to try to make it numeric in SAS.

SAS for R Users: A Book for Data Scientists, First Edition. Ajay Ohri.
© 2020 John Wiley & Sons, Inc. Published 2020 by John Wiley & Sons, Inc.

```
data ajay21;
set ajay2;
a2=1*a;
run;

proc print data=ajay21;
Run;
Obs      a                a2
1        1234567          1234567

proc contents data=ajay21;
run;
#       Variable      Type      Len
1       a             Char      7
2       a2            Num       8
```

We also use input to convert character to numeric variable, but in SAS we need to specify the correct type of informat as well.

COMMA ELIMINATION USING INFORMAT

```
data new3;
char_var = '8,000,000';
numeric_var = input(char_var,comma10.);
run;

Proc print data=new3;
Run;

Obs      char_var        numeric_var
1        8,000,000       8000000
```

DOLLAR AND COMMA ELIMINATION USING INFORMAT

```
data new4;
char_var = '$9,000,000';
numeric_var = input(char_var,dollar10.);
run;

proc print data=new4;
Run;

Obs      char_var        numeric_var
1        $9,000,000      9000000
```

NUMERIC TO CHARACTER USING PUT

```
data test ;
prodID = 011 ;
result = put(prodID , 3.) ;
run ;

proc print data=test;
run;
Obs      prodID     result
1        11         11

proc contents data=test;
run;

#       Variable     Type      Len
1       prodID       Num       8
2       result       Char      3
```

4.1.2   Numeric Data in R

Using R As Calculator

```
#addition
>5+71
[1]  76

#exponential
>5^3
[1]125

#modulo or remainder
>35%%3
[1]  2
```

Assignment Of Numeric Values

```
>x=15
>x
[1]  15

>y=115.75
>y

[1]  115.75
```

Arithmetic with Numeric Variables

```
>z=y-x

>z
[1]  100.75

>y%%x
[1]  10.75
```

Numeric Vector

```
>numeric_vec=c(11,-5,10,18)

>numeric_vec
[1]  1 -5 10 8
```

Naming A Vector

```
>names(numeric_vec)= c("january", "february", "march", "april")

>numeric_vec

january  february  march  april
11         -5        10     18
```

Convert Numeric to String

```
> ab=4:8
> ab
[1]  4 5 6 7 8

> ac=as.character(ab)
> class(ac)
[1]  "character"

> ac
[1]  "4" "5" "6" "7" "8"

> ad=as.numeric(ac)
> ad
[1]  4 5 6 7 8
> class(ad)
[1]  "numeric"
```

4.2   Working with Date Data

Dates are a special case of numeric data because dates have multiple formats. Date variables can pose a challenge in data management. Date data are quite critical for industries like finance, telecom, sales etc. R and SAS provide several options for dealing with date and datetime data.

4.2.1   Handling Dates in SAS

SAS date value is a value that represents the number of days between 1 January 1960, and a specified date. Dates before 1 January 1960, are negative numbers; dates after are positive numbers. Various SAS language elements handle SAS date values: functions, formats and informats.

READING DATE
The format used here is date9. which is used when specifying the first three letters of month, in total making it nine characters.

```
data new1;
maindate = "12JUL2017";
date = input(maindate,date9.);
format date date9.;
Run;

proc print data=new1;
Run;

Obs    maindate      date
1      12JUL2017     12JUL2017

proc contents data=new1;
run;

#      Variable    Type     Len     Format
2      date        Num      8       DATE9.
1      maindate    Char     9
```

DATE9. is an INFORMAT. In an INPUT statement, it provides the SAS interpreter with a set of translation commands it can send to the compiler to turn your text into the right numbers, which will then look like a date once the right FORMAT is applied.

INFORMAT tells the compiler how to read data while FORMAT tells the compiler how to write data. FORMATs are just visible representations of numbers (or characters).

Changing Date Formats

By default, ddmmyy. reads seven characters. To specify year with century use ddmmyy10.

```
data new2;
maindate = "12JUL2018";
date = input(maindate,date9.);
format date ddmmyy.
Run;

proc print data=new2;
run;

Obs     maindate      date
1       12JUL2018     12/07/18
```

Calculating Differences Between Dates

Here today() in SAS is like Sys.Date() in R. We simply subtract dates in SAS (instead of using difftime in R)

```
data dates_diff;
format dob date9. b date9.;
dob=input("7jun1977",date9.);
b=today();
c=dob-b;
run;

proc print data=dates_diff;
Run;

Obs     dob           b            c
1       01APR1977     09DEC2018    15227
```

Using Intck Option

We can use datepart to extract date and use intck to obtain difference in dates

```
data new3;
format a1 b1 date9.;
a0='01jan2009:00:00:00'dt;
b0='01jan2012:00:00:00'dt;
a1=datepart(a0);
```

```
b1=datepart(b0);
days=intck('day',a1,b1);
run;

proc print data=NEW3;
run;

Obs    a1            b1          a0           b0           days
1      01JAN2009  01JAN2012  1546387200  1640995200  1095

proc contents data=NEW3;
run;

# Variable     Type     Len      Format
3    a0         Num      8
1    a1         Num      8        DATE9.
4    b0         Num      8
2    b1         Num      8        DATE9.
5    days       Num      8
```

4.2.2 Handling Dates in R

Having your dates in the proper format allows R to know that they are dates, and what calculations it should perform on them.

The builtin as.Date function handles dates (without times). The as.Date function allows a variety of input formats through the format = argument.

The default format is a four-digit year, followed by a month, then a day, separated by either dashes or slashes.

```
>as.Date("2018-06-16")
[1]"2018-06-16"
> as.Date('16 June 2018',format="%d %B %Y")
#%d consists of the day, %B consists of full month name and
%Y contains the year with century.
[1]  "2018-06-16"
```

Consider another example for the usage of format option in as.Date function.

```
>strDates <- c("01/05/1965", "08/16/1975")
>dates <- as.Date(strDates, "%m/%d/%Y")
>dates
[1] "1965-01-05" "1975-08-16"
```

tz option is used to specify a time zone.

```
> Sys.timezone()
[1] "Asia/Calcutta"
> test1 <- as.Date ( "2016-01-01" , tz =" Asia/Calcutta" )
> test1
[1] "2016-01-01"
```

CONVERTING DATE TO NUMERIC VALUE

R stores dates using 1 January 1970 as the origin. When R looks at dates as integers it calculates the days passed since 1 January 1970.

```
> y<-as.Date('1977-04-01')

> z<-as.numeric(y)

> z
[1] 2647

> class(z)
[1] "numeric"
```

CONVERTING DATE TO CHARACTER VALUE

```
>x<-as.character(y)
>x
[1] "1970-01-01"
>class(x)
[1] "character"
```

USING Sys.Date FUNCTION

To get the current date, the Sys.Date function will return a Date object.

```
> Sys.Date()
[1] "2018-12-09"
```

Using Posixct Function

Date and time are stored using POSIXct function but it can parse only the format of YYYY-MM-DD HH:MM:SS. strptime is used for different formats.

The formatting and order variations of the date pieces is what **strptime** deals with so as.POSIXct can recognize the date.

```
> Sys.Date()
[1] "2018-12-09"

> Sys.time()
[1] "2018-12-09 12:33:20 IST"

> as.POSIXct(Sys.Date())
[1] "2018-12-09 05:30:00 IST"

> as.POSIXct(strptime("09/12/2018 12:33", format = "%d/%m/%Y
%H:%M"), tz ="Asia/Calcutta")

[1] "2018-12-09 12:33:00 IST"
```

Giving Time Differences Between Two Dates using **difftime**

```
> test1<-as.Date("2018-01-01", tz="UTC")
> test2<-strptime("2016-01-25", format="%Y-%m-%d", tz="UTC")

> result=difftime(as.POSIXct(test2), as.POSIXct(test1,tz="UTC"),
units="days")

> result
Time difference of -707 days
```

Lubridate Package

R is greatly simplified and augmented by the **lubridate** package. It has many functions but primarily the format either says 'dmy', 'mdy', "ymd" which can be easily used in R.

```
> library(lubridate)

> a='1Jan2018'
> dmy(a)
[1] "2018-01-01"

> b='1/21/18'
> mdy(b)
[1] "2018-01-21"
```

```
> c='1-January-2017'
> dmy(c)

[1] "2017-01-01"
```

Giving Time Differences using Lubridate Package

```
> adob="21 June 1977"
> adob2=dmy(adob)
> adob2
[1] "1977-06-21"

> mydob="15 June 1981"
> mydob2=dmy(mydob)
> mydob2
[1] "1981-06-15"

> difftime(adob2,mydob2,units="days")
Time difference of -1455 days
```

4.3   Handling Strings Data

A vast amount data is in the form of text particularly emails, documents and the Internet. The ability to manipulate string data types is critical to a data scientist.

A "string" is a collection of characters that make up one element of a vector. You can tell a string because it will be mostly be enclosed in (double) quotation marks.

4.3.1   Handling Strings Data in SAS

Assigning String Values to Variables

```
data string;
LENGTH string1 $ 6 String2 $ 5;
/*String variables of length 6 and 5 */
String1 = 'hi';
String2 = 'user';
 run;
proc print data=string;
Run;

Obs      string1      String2
1        hi           user
```

```
Data names;
INPUT name $30.;
DATALINES; /* here we have used to separate the first name,
middle name ,last name */
a b c
Ajay singh ohri
lora Marie
;
run;

proc print data=names;
Run;

Obs     name
1       a b c
2       Ajay singh ohri
3       lora Marie
```

Using SUBSTRN option

```
data substring;
length string string1 string2 $12;
string="Hello World";
string1 = substrn(String,3,4) ; /*Extract from position 3 to 7 (3+4) */
string2 = substrn(String,4) ;/*Extract from position 4 onwards */
run;

proc print data = substring ;
run;

Obs    string          string1    string2
1      Hello World     llo        lo World
```

Using Trimn Function

```
data string;
LENGTH str1 $ 12 ;
  str1='Hello World';
    length1 = lengthc(Str1);
    length_trim2 = lengthc(TRIMN(str1));
  run;

proc print data=string;
run;

Obs     str1            length1    length_trim2
1       Hello World     12         11
```

CONCATENATION OF STRING

```
DATA abc;
INPUT abc1 $char3. abc2 $char3. ;
DATALINES;
ab cd
;
run;

DATA result;
SET abc;
concate=abc1||abc2;
run;

proc print data=result;
Run;


Obs     abc1      abc2      concate
1       ab        cd        ab cd
```

```
data string1;
LENGTH string1 $ 6 String2 $ 5;
/*String variables of length 6 and 5 */
String1 = 'hi';
String2 = 'user';
combined_string = String1||String2 ;
run;

proc print data=string1;
Run;


Obs     string1      String2      combined_string
1       hi           user         hi user
```

TO CONVERT CHARACTER TO NUMERIC

```
data new;
char = '1234567';
numeric = input(char, 8.);
Run;

proc contents data=new;
run;


#       Variable      Type      Len
1       char          Char      7
2       numeric       Num       8
```

```
proc print data=new;
Run;


Obs     char          numeric
1       1234567       1234567
```

Replace One Value of String with Another- Here, **translate** function replaces a with &

```
data a;
input x $40.;
x1=translate(x,'a','&');
cards;
My&Name&IS&akansha
Hello&World
;
Run;

proc print data=a;
Run;

Obs    x       x1
1      My&Name&IS&akansha      MyaNameaISaakansha
2      Hello&World   HelloaWorld
```

Eliminating Whitespace using **compress**

```
data a;
input x $40.;
cards;
"My&Name &IS &akansha"
"Hello & World"
;
Run;

data a2;
set a;
x1=compress(x,' ');
run;

proc print data=a2;
run;

Obs    x                            x1
1      "My&Name &IS &akansha"       "My&Name&IS&akansha"
2      "Hello & World"              "Hello&World"
```

4.3.2 Handling Strings Data in R

In R, a piece of text is represented as a sequence of characters (letters, numbers, and symbols). The data type R provided for storing sequences of characters is **character**. Formally, the mode of an object that holds character strings in R is "character".

You express character strings by surrounding text within double quotes or single quotes.

ASSIGNING STRING VALUE TO AN OBJECT:

```
>a='this is a string'>a
[1] "this is a string"
>b="A string won't omit quotes"
>b
[1] "A string won't omit quotes"
```

SPECIAL CHARACTERS IN STRINGS

```
>a="Tab\t"
>a

[1] "Tab\t"
```

PRINT FORMATTED STRING

```
>cat ("Tab\t")

[1] Tab
```

COUNTING CHARACTERS IN STRING

```
>nchar ("Tab\t")
[1] 5
```

VECTOR STRINGS

```
>str <- letters[1:5]
>str
[1] "a" "b" "c" "d" "e"
>mean (str)
## Warning in mean.default(str): argument is not numeric or
logical: returning NA
[1] NA
```

USING EXTRACTION AND ASSIGNMENT OPERATORS

```
>str[3:4] <- c("Yes", "No")
>str
[1] "a" "b" "Yes" "No" "e"
>length(str)
[1] 5
```

CONVERTING NUMERIC TO STRINGS

```
>str <- c("1", "2", "Yes", "No", "5")
>as.numeric(str)
## Warning: NAs introduced by coercion
[1] 1 2 NA NA 5
#you can turn the warning options off with the options() command
```

PARSING STRINGS TOGETHER

```
>paste (c("a", "b", "c"), 1:5, sep="")
[1] "a1" "b2" "c3" "a4" "b5"
>paste (1:3, c(10, 20, 30), sep=" which is ")
[1] "1 which is 10" "2 which is 20" "3 which is 30"
```

BREAKING A STRING AT A DELIMITER

```
>strsplit ("Nospaces", "s")
[[1]]
[1] "No" "pace"
```

USING DescTools, trimws IN R ELIMINATES WHITE SPACE

```
>library(DescTools)
>x=" abcdfd "
>x
[1] " abcdfd "
>trimws(x,which = c("both"))

[1] "abcdfd"
```

STRING TO NUMERIC

```
>x = factor(4:8)
>aa=as.character(x)
>class(x)
[1] "factor"
>ab= as.numeric(aa)
>ab
[1] 4 5 6 7 8
>class(ab)

[1] "numeric"
```

Note R has another data type called factor which is used for categorical variables. They may look like string data but usually have a few levels and are identified as factor variables in R. In SAS they would be character and analyzed using Proc Freq.

4.4 Quiz Questions

1 How do you create a vector in R?

2 Give the function used to name the vector elements.

3 Name the functions used to convert numeric data type to character data type in R.

4 How can you simplify date handling in R?

5 Give the name of function to calculate the difference between two dates in R?

6 Give the name of function to calculate the difference between two dates in SAS?

7 Give three different types of date format and their syntax in SAS.

8 Calculate the characters in string "R and SAS" in R.

9 Concatenate the strings "Hello" and "World" in SAS and R.

10 What is the command used to eliminate white space in R.

11 Name a package in R that handles strings data.

Quiz Answers

1 Vectors are created using c() command.

2 names(vector_name) command is used to name the elements of a vector.

3 In R: as.character.

4 Date handling can be simplified using lubridate function.

5 In R: difftime

6 In SAS: intck

7 17-07-18 ddmmyy8., 07–17-18 mmddyy8., 17jul2018 date9.

8 >nchar("R and SAS")

9 In R: paste("Hello", "World", sep=" ") In SAS:

```
Data strings;
Input first $ second $;
Datalines;
Hello World
;
Run;

Data concatenate;
Set strings;
combined=first||second;
          Run;
```

10 Using DescTools package, trimws command eliminates whitespace in R. We can also use gsub (gsub(" ",dataframe$variable))

11 stringr package

5

Numerical Summary and Groupby Analysis

We use numerical summary methods to see measures of central tendency (mean, median(and dispersion (variance, standard deviation) as well as other measures (skewness, kurtosis) and distributions (max,min, interquartile range) to find estimated and expected values for analysis of numerical variables. We use groupby to slice and dice the data for further analysis. In R we have the concept of tidy data:

1) Each variable forms a column.
2) Each observation forms a row.
3) Each type of observational unit forms a table

By default all datasets in SAS are tidy.
Also in R we have the concept of Split-Apply-Combine. Split Apply Combine refers to the following

1) split data into pieces,
2) apply some function to each piece,
3) combine the results back together again

5.1 Numerical Summary and Groupby Analysis

Here we use different functions and procedures to do analysis on numerical data.

5.2 Numerical Summary and Groupby Analysis in SAS

In SAS – we use the class statement for grouping and var statement for specifying for a particular value-

- proc means,

SAS for R Users: A Book for Data Scientists, First Edition. Ajay Ohri.
© 2020 John Wiley & Sons, Inc. Published 2020 by John Wiley & Sons, Inc.

Proc means is one of the most common procedure used for analyzing the data. It calculates descriptive statistics like Mean, Standard Deviation, Maximum and Minimum along with Number of observations. By default, proc means displays the default Statistics: It can be customized for other descriptive statistics.

Note sashelp library in SAS is like the default datasets library in R, as both give test datasets for learning.

```
proc means data=sashelp.cars;
Run;
```

The MEANS Procedure

Variable	Label	N	Mean	Std Dev	Minimum	Maximum
MSRP		428	32774.86	19431.72	10280.00	192465.00
Invoice		428	30014.70	17642.12	9875.00	173560.00
EngineSize	Engine Size (L)	428	3.1967290	1.1085947	1.3000000	8.3000000
Cylinders		426	5.8075117	1.5584426	3.0000000	12.0000000
Horsepower		428	215.8855140	71.8360316	73.0000000	500.0000000
MPG_City	MPG (City)	428	20.0607477	5.2382176	10.0000000	60.0000000
MPG_Highway	MPG (Highway)	428	26.8434579	5.7412007	12.0000000	66.0000000
Weight	Weight (LBS)	428	3577.95	758.9832146	1850.00	7190.00
Wheelbase	Wheelbase (IN)	428	108.1542056	8.3118130	89.0000000	144.0000000
Length	Length (IN)	428	186.3621495	14.3579913	143.0000000	238.0000000

2) We can now check for custom statistics using proc means. Note we used max-dec for controlling number of decimal points, where as **min, p25, median, p75, max** are the five numbers for exploratory data analysis (minimum, first quartile, median, third quartile, and maximum respectively)

```
proc means data=sashelp.cars min p25 median p75 max MAXDEC=1;
run;
```

Variable	Label	Minimum	25th Pctl	Median	75th Pctl	Maximum
MSRP		10280.0	20329.5	27635.0	39215.0	192465.0
Invoice		9875.0	18851.0	25294.5	35732.5	173560.0
EngineSize	Engine Size (L)	1.3	2.3	3.0	3.9	8.3
Cylinders		3.0	4.0	6.0	6.0	12.0
Horsepower		73.0	165.0	210.0	255.0	500.0
MPG_City	MPG (City)	10.0	17.0	19.0	21.5	60.0
MPG_Highway	MPG (Highway)	12.0	24.0	26.0	29.0	66.0
Weight	Weight (LBS)	1850.0	3103.0	3474.5	3978.5	7190.0
Wheelbase	Wheelbase (IN)	89.0	103.0	107.0	112.0	144.0
Length	Length (IN)	143.0	178.0	187.0	194.0	238.0

Suppose we want to find the mean of one variable (say invoice) but grouped by different regions to see the difference in invoices across origin

The code used class (to class by certain variable Y) and uses var (to get only that variable not the entire numerical variables)

```
proc means data=sashelp.cars mean;
var invoice;
class origin;
Run;
Analysis Variable:  : Invoice
Origin      N Obs     Mean
Asia        158       22602.18
Europe      123       44395.08
USA         147       25949.34
```

But without the class statement it gives entire mean of variable

```
proc means data=sashelp.cars mean;
var invoice;
/* class origin; */
Run;

Analysis Variable: Invoice
Mean
30014.70
```

- proc summary,- it is quite similar to Proc means except it can compute statistics for data across all observations or within groups of observations (as per SAS Documentation).

```
proc summary data=sashelp.cars mean print;
Class origin;
var invoice;
run;
```

The SUMMARY Procedure

Analysis Variable: Invoice

Origin	N Obs	Mean
Asia	158	22 602.18
Europe	123	44 395.08
USA	147	25 949.34

- proc univariate does a comprehensive analysis on the variable

```
proc univariate data=sashelp.cars;
var invoice;
run;
```

The UNIVARIATE Procedure

Variable: Invoice

Moments

N	428	Sum Weights	428
Mean	30014.7009	Sum Observations	12846292
Std Deviation	17642.1178	Variance	311244319
Skewness	2.8347404	Kurtosis	13.9461638
Uncorrected SS	5.18479E11	Corrected SS	1.32901E11
Coeff Variation	58.778256	Std Error Mean	852.763949

Basic Statistical Measures

Location		Variability	
Mean	30014.70	Std Deviation	17642
Median	25294.50	Variance	311244319
Mode	14207.00	Range	163685
		Interquartile Range	16882

Note: The mode displayed is the smallest of 3 modes with a count of 2.

Tests for Location: Mu0 = 0

Test	Statistic		p Value	
Student's t	t	35.19696	$Pr > \|t\|$	<0.0001
Sign	M	214	$Pr >= \|M\|$	<0.0001
Signed Rank	S	45903	$Pr >= \|S\|$	<0.0001

Quantiles (Definition 5)

Level	Quantile
100% Max	173560.0
99%	88324.0
95%	66830.0
90%	48377.0
75% Q3	35732.5
50% Median	25294.5

(Continued)

Quantiles (Definition 5)

Level	Quantile
25% Q1	18851.0
10%	14375.0
5%	12830.0
1%	10642.0
0% Min	9875.0

Extreme Observations

Lowest		Highest	
Value	Obs	Value	Obs
9875	207	88324	262
10107	169	113388	271
10144	383	117854	272
10319	346	119600	263
10642	385	173560	335

With option **plot** it makes graphs for distribution and probability plots

```
proc univariate data=sashelp.cars plot ;
var invoice;
run;
```

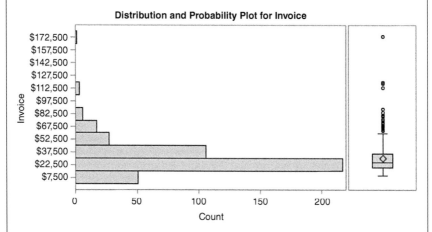

Figure 5.1 Proc Univariate Output.

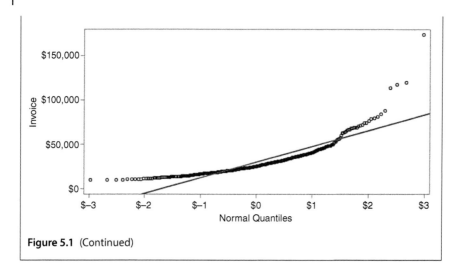

Figure 5.1 (Continued)

- proc tabulate,

In proc tabulate we can do multiple numerical analysis within the same table. Note, however, the slightly different way of syntax in proc tabulate compared to proc means.

```
proc tabulate data=sashelp.cars ;
class origin;
var invoice;
table origin*invoice*mean;
run;

               Origin
Asia           Europe       USA
Invoice        Invoice      Invoice
Mean           Mean         Mean
22602.18       44395.08     25949.34


Another example

PROC TABULATE DATA=sashelp.cars;
CLASS Make Model ;
var Invoice;
TABLE Make, Invoice*mean;
RUN;

Note: In output below, we have truncated and removed some rows to enable it
to fit it in the book
```

	Invoice
	Mean
Acura	38 590.86
Audi	39 330.11
BMW	39 620.65
Buick	27 854.89
Cadillac	46 426.88
Chevrolet	24 060.81
Chrysler	25 270.07
Dodge	24 160.08
Ford	21 953.00

- proc report is a combination of **PRINT, MEANS,** and **TABULATE procedures.**
- proc freq is used for categorical variables (we will refer to this in the next chapter)
- Proc sql enables us to use SQL syntax with SAS. We can use this to obtain statistics as well as for doing group by analysis.
- Proc sort is used to sort the data. Using option nodupkey enables only unique values as duplicate keys are deleted.

```
data cars;
set sashelp.cars;
run;

proc sql;
select count(type),type,origin
from cars
group by type ,origin;
run;

        Origin
158     Asia
123     Europe
147     USA

proc sql;
select avg(mpg_city),origin
from cars
group by origin;
run;
```

```
          Origin
22.01266  Asia
18.73171  Europe
19.07483  USA

proc sql;
select max(mpg_city),origin
from cars
group by origin;
Run;

      Origin
60    Asia
38    Europe
29    USA
```

Note to get **a random subset** in SAS we can use the ranuni function as follows

```
data cars;
set sashelp.cars;
run;

NOTE: There were 428 observations read from the data set SASHELP.CARS.
NOTE: The data set WORK.CARS has 428 observations and 15 variables.

data cars2;
set sashelp.cars;
where ranuni(12)<.2;
Run;

NOTE: There were 82 observations read from the data set SASHELP.CARS.

   WHERE RANUNI(12) < 0.2;

NOTE: The data set WORK.CARS2 has 82 observations and 15 variables.
```

5.3 Numerical Summary and Group by Analysis in R

In R, the **summary** function gives a lucid example of summarizing the entire datasets. It also gives frequency tabulations of categorical variables

```
> summary(iris)
 Sepal.Length    Sepal.Width     Petal.Length    Petal.Width          Species  
 Min.   :4.300   Min.   :2.000   Min.   :1.000   Min.   :0.100   setosa    :50  
 1st Qu.:5.100   1st Qu.:2.800   1st Qu.:1.600   1st Qu.:0.300   versicolor:50  
 Median :5.800   Median :3.000   Median :4.350   Median :1.300   virginica :50  
 Mean   :5.843   Mean   :3.057   Mean   :3.758   Mean   :1.199                  
 3rd Qu.:6.400   3rd Qu.:3.300   3rd Qu.:5.100   3rd Qu.:1.800                  
 Max.   :7.900   Max.   :4.400   Max.   :6.900   Max.   :2.500                  
```

We can also use lapply to apply functions to a list:

```
> lapply(iris[1:4], summary)

$`Sepal.Length`
  Min.  1st Qu.  Median   Mean  3rd Qu.   Max.
 4.300  5.100    5.800   5.843  6.400    7.900

$Sepal.Width
  Min.  1st Qu.  Median   Mean  3rd Qu.   Max.
 2.000  2.800    3.000   3.057  3.300    4.400

$Petal.Length
  Min.  1st Qu.  Median   Mean  3rd Qu.   Max.
 1.000  1.600    4.350   3.758  5.100    6.900

$Petal.Width
  Min.  1st Qu.  Median   Mean  3rd Qu.   Max.
 0.100  0.300    1.300   1.199  1.800    2.500
```

5.3.1 Hmisc and Data.Table Packages

The HMisc package in R has many functions for numeric analysis including describe and summarize. Here the **describe** function gives univariate distribution analysis just like Proc Univariate in SAS (here of Sepal Length in iris) while **summarize** can do group by analysis here – Sepal.Length median grouped by Species). Describe is also a more elaborative function than summary in R, but a much more concise equivalent to proc univariate in SAS.

```
> describe(iris$Sepal.Length)
iris$Sepal.Length
    n missing distinct   Info  Mean   Gmd    .05    .10    .25    .50    .75    .90    .95
  150       0       35  0.998 5.843 0.9462 4.600 4.800 5.100 5.800 6.400 6.900 7.255

lowest : 4.3 4.4 4.5 4.6 4.7, highest: 7.3 7.4 7.6 7.7 7.9

> summarize(iris$Sepal.Length,iris$Species,median)
  iris$Species iris$Sepal.Length
1       setosa               5.0
2   versicolor               5.9
3    virginica               6.5
```

The **data.table** packages enables you to both read data fast (using the function fread which is much better than read,.csv) but also calculates on it very quicklt. A data.table is a special case of data frame. Operations on data. table use three parameters i,j,k

DT [I,J,K]

Take DT, subset/reorder rows using I, then calculate J, grouped by K

```
>library(data.table)
>dt = as.data.table(iris)

> dt[,mean(Sepal.Length), Species]

    Species    V1
1: setosa      5.006
2: versicolor 5.936
3: virginica  6.588

> dt[Sepal.Length>6,mean(Sepal.Length), Species]
    Species    V1
1: versicolor 6.450000
2: virginica  6.778049
```

Object.size gives the size occupied by an object

```
> object.size(dt)
8200 bytes
```

tables(): shows all data.tables in memory, space occupied, their columns with keys if any.

```
> tables()
NAME           NROW     NCOL  MB             COLS              KEY
1: a           61       5     0  Sepal.Length,Sepal.Width,Petal.
                                    Length,Petal.Width,Species
2: diamonds 53,940     10     3  carat,cut,color,clarity,depth,
                                    table,...
3: dt         150       5     0  Sepal.Length,Sepal.Width,Petal.
                                    Length,Petal.Width,Species Species
4: iris       150       5     0  Sepal.Length,Sepal.Width,Petal.
                                    Length,Petal.Width,Species Species

Total: 3MB
```

sessionInfo(): It collects information about the Current R Session including packages attached.

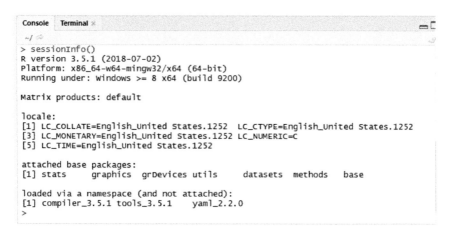

```
Console  Terminal ×
~/
> sessionInfo()
R version 3.5.1 (2018-07-02)
Platform: x86_64-w64-mingw32/x64 (64-bit)
Running under: Windows >= 8 x64 (build 9200)

Matrix products: default

locale:
[1] LC_COLLATE=English_United States.1252  LC_CTYPE=English_United States.1252
[3] LC_MONETARY=English_United States.1252 LC_NUMERIC=C
[5] LC_TIME=English_United States.1252

attached base packages:
[1] stats     graphics  grDevices utils     datasets  methods   base

loaded via a namespace (and not attached):
[1] compiler_3.5.1 tools_3.5.1    yaml_2.2.0
>
```

Figure 5.2 sessionInfo Output in R.

5.3.2 Dplyr Package

dplyr: dplyr is a powerful R-package to transform and summarize tabular data. It contains functions which perform data manipulation. The following functions from select to sample_n are from dplyr packages which needs to be loaded before they can be accessed.

Select helps to select a few columns by name

```
> library(dplyr)
> data("iris")
> a=select(iris,Species,Petal.Length,Sepal.Length)

> str(a)
'data.frame':	150 obs. of 3 variables:
 $ Species     : Factor w/ 3 levels "setosa","versicolor",..: 1 1 1 1 1 1 1 1 1 1 ...
 $ Petal.Length: num 1.4 1.4 1.3 1.5 1.4 1.7 1.4 1.5 1.4 1.5 ...
 $ Sepal.Length: num 5.1 4.9 4.7 4.6 5 5.4 4.6 5 4.4 4.9 ...
```

To select a range of columns, we can also use the (:) colon operator.

```
> a=select(iris,Species,Petal.Length:Sepal.Length)

> str(a)
'data.frame':	150 obs. of 4 variables:
 $ Species     : Factor w/ 3 levels "setosa","versicolor",..: 1 1 1 1 1 1 1 1 1 1 ...
 $ Petal.Length: num 1.4 1.4 1.3 1.5 1.4 1.7 1.4 1.5 1.4 1.5 ...
 $ Sepal.Width : num 3.5 3 3.2 3.1 3.6 3.9 3.4 3.4 2.9 3.1 ...
 $ Sepal.Length: num 5.1 4.9 4.7 4.6 5 5.4 4.6 5 4.4 4.9 ...
```

To select all the columns except a specific column or rather to drop a column , we can use the "-"
(subtraction) operator .This is negative indexing.

```
> b=select(iris,-Species)
> str(b)
'data.frame':   150 obs. of 4 variables:
$ Sepal.Length: num 5.1 4.9 4.7 4.6 5 5.4 4.6 5 4.4 4.9 ...
$ Sepal.Width : num 3.5 3 3.2 3.1 3.6 3.9 3.4 3.4 2.9 3.1 ...
$ Petal.Length: num 1.4 1.4 1.3 1.5 1.4 1.7 1.4 1.5 1.4 1.5 ...
$ Petal.Width : num 0.2 0.2 0.2 0.2 0.2 0.4 0.3 0.2 0.2 0.1 ...

Multiple columns can be dropped as well
> b=select(iris,-Species,-Sepal.Length)
> str(b)
'data.frame':   150 obs. of 3 variables:
$ Sepal.Width : num 3.5 3 3.2 3.1 3.6 3.9 3.4 3.4 2.9 3.1 ...
$ Petal.Length: num 1.4 1.4 1.3 1.5 1.4 1.7 1.4 1.5 1.4 1.5 ...
$ Petal.Width : num 0.2 0.2 0.2 0.2 0.2 0.4 0.3 0.2 0.2 0.1 ...
```

filter: It filters the dataset by condition.

```
> str(iris)
'data.frame':    150 obs. of  5 variables:
 $ Sepal.Length: num  5.1 4.9 4.7 4.6 5 5.4 4.6 5 4.4 4.9 ...
 $ Sepal.Width : num  3.5 3 3.2 3.1 3.6 3.9 3.4 3.4 2.9 3.1 ...
 $ Petal.Length: num  1.4 1.4 1.3 1.5 1.4 1.7 1.4 1.5 1.4 1.5 ...
 $ Petal.Width : num  0.2 0.2 0.2 0.2 0.2 0.4 0.3 0.2 0.2 0.1 ...
 $ Species     : Factor w/ 3 levels "setosa","versicolor",..: 1 1 1 1 1 1 1 1 1 1 ...

> d=filter(iris,Petal.Width>1)
> str(d)
'data.frame':    93 obs. of  5 variables:
 $ Sepal.Length: num  7 6.4 6.9 5.5 6.5 5.7 6.3 6.6 5.2 5.9 ...
 $ Sepal.Width : num  3.2 3.2 3.1 2.3 2.8 2.8 3.3 2.9 2.7 3 ...
 $ Petal.Length: num  4.7 4.5 4.9 4 4.6 4.5 4.7 4.6 3.9 4.2 ...
 $ Petal.Width : num  1.4 1.5 1.5 1.3 1.5 1.3 1.6 1.3 1.4 1.5 ...
 $ Species     : Factor w/ 3 levels "setosa","versicolor",..: 2 2 2 2 2 2 2 2 2 2 ...
```

In SAS we can choose data by row numbers using _N_

```
data iris2;
  set sashelp.iris;
  if _N_ in (2, 6, 8, 10, 34) then output;
  run;

proc print data= iris2 ;
  run;
```

Obs	Species	SepalLength	SepalWidth	PetalLength	PetalWidth
1	Setosa	46	34	14	3
2	Setosa	48	31	16	2
3	Setosa	49	36	14	1
4	Setosa	50	35	16	6
5	Setosa	47	32	13	2

Slice: This dplyr function shows selected columns (or range of columns) by their position.

```
> slice(iris,10:15)

  Sepal.Length Sepal.Width Petal.Length Petal.Width Species
1     4.9          3.1          1.5         0.1      setosa
2     5.4          3.7          1.5         0.2      setosa
3     4.8          3.4          1.6         0.2      setosa
4     4.8          3.0          1.4         0.1      setosa
5     4.3          3.0          1.1         0.1      setosa
6     5.8          4.0          1.2         0.2      setosa
```

In SAS Proc Sort helps to sort the data:

```
proc sort data=sashelp.iris out=iris;
by SepalLength;
run;

proc print data=iris (obs=5);
Run;
```

Obs	Species	SepalLength	SepalWidth	PetalLength	PetalWidth
1	Setosa	43	30	11	1
2	Setosa	44	32	13	2
3	Setosa	44	30	13	2
4	Setosa	44	29	14	2
5	Setosa	45	23	13	3

Arrange: This dplyr function helps to sort the data:

```
> c=arrange(iris,Petal.Length)

> slice(c,10:20)

     Sepal.Length Sepal.Width Petal.Length Petal.Width Species
1    4.5          2.3         1.3          0.3         setosa
2    4.4          3.2         1.3          0.2         setosa
3    5.1          3.5         1.4          0.2         setosa
4    4.9          3.0         1.4          0.2         setosa
5    5.0          3.6         1.4          0.2         setosa
6    4.6          3.4         1.4          0.3         setosa
7    4.4          2.9         1.4          0.2         setosa
8    4.8          3.0         1.4          0.1         setosa
9    5.1          3.5         1.4          0.3         setosa
10   5.2          3.4         1.4          0.2         setosa
11   5.5          4.2         1.4          0.2         setosa
>
```

In SAS we can create new columns like below in the Data step:

```
data iris;
set sashelp.iris;
ratio=SepalLength/SepalWidth;
run;

proc print data= iris (obs=5);
run;

Obs Species SepalLength SepalWidth PetalLength PetalWidth ratio
1    Setosa  50          33          14          2          1.51515
2    Setosa  46          34          14          3          1.35294
3    Setosa  46          36          10          2          1.27778
4    Setosa  51          33          17          5          1.54545
5    Setosa  55          35          13          2          1.57143
```

Mutate: This dplyr function creates new columns/variables.

```
> d=mutate(iris,ratio=Sepal.Length/Sepal.Width)

> head(d)
  Sepal.Length Sepal.Width Petal.Length Petal.Width Species ratio
1 5.1          3.5         1.4          0.2         setosa  1.457143
2 4.9          3.0         1.4          0.2         setosa  1.633333
3 4.7          3.2         1.3          0.2         setosa  1.468750
4 4.6          3.1         1.5          0.2         setosa  1.483871
5 5.0          3.6         1.4          0.2         setosa  1.388889
6 5.4          3.9         1.7          0.4         setosa  1.384615
```

In SAS, to keep only a certain variable we include it in KEEP = function. Or we can drop variables using DROP = function.

```
data iris (keep=ratio);
set sashelp.iris;
ratio=SepalLength/SepalWidth;
run;

proc print data = iris (obs=5);
Run;

Obs    ratio
1      1.51515
2      1.35294
3      1.27778
4      1.54545
5      1.57143
```

transmute(): This dplyr function removes existing variables preserving only the new one.

```
> d=transmute(iris,ratio=Sepal.Length/Sepal.Width)
> head(d)
  ratio
1 1.457143
2 1.633333
3 1.468750
4 1.483871
5 1.388889
6 1.384615
```

summarise(): creates summary statistics for a given column:

```
> summarise(iris,mean(Sepal.Length))

 mean(Sepal.Length)
1      5.843333
```

group_by(): takes an existing data frame and converts it into a grouped data-frame where operations can be performed "by group".

```
> g=group_by(iris,Species)

> summarise(g,mean(Sepal.Length))

# A tibble: 3 x 2

 Species       `mean(Sepal.Length)`
 <fct>          <dbl>
1 setosa         5.01
2 versicolor     5.94
3 virginica      6.59
```

sample_n(): Random n rows from data (10 rows for example selected at random). Similar to ranuni in SAS. In addition **sample_frac** returns random rows as fractional value of total rows (0.1 will be 10% of total rows). You can see by the row numbers below that they are random rows.

```
> sample_n(iris,10)
      Sepal.Length Sepal.Width Petal.Length Petal.Width Species
124 6.3                2.7         4.9          1.8      virginica
103 7.1                3.0         5.9          2.1      virginica
128 6.1                3.0         4.9          1.8      virginica
87  6.7                3.1         4.7          1.5      versicolor
120 6.0                2.2         5.0          1.5      virginica
12  4.8                3.4         1.6          0.2      setosa
50  5.0                3.3         1.4          0.2      setosa
41  5.0                3.5         1.3          0.3      setosa
107    4.9      2.5     4.5      1.7    virginica
63     6.0      2.2     4.0      1.0    versicolor
```

```
> sample_frac(iris,0.1)
    Sepal.Length Sepal.Width Petal.Length Petal.Width Species
134 6.3              2.8          5.1          1.5     virginica
18  5.1              3.5          1.4          0.3     setosa
148 6.5              3.0          5.2          2.0     virginica
95  5.6              2.7          4.2          1.3     versicolor
96  5.7              3.0          4.2          1.2     versicolor
61  5.0              2.0          3.5          1.0     versicolor
77  6.8              2.8          4.8          1.4     versicolor
127 6.2              2.8          4.8          1.8     virginica
25  4.8              3.4          1.9          0.2     setosa
42  4.5              2.3          1.3          0.3     setosa
71  5.9              3.2          4.8          1.8     versicolor
78  6.7              3.0          5.0          1.7     versicolor
105 6.5              3.0          5.8          2.2     virginica
17  5.4              3.9          1.3          0.4     setosa
102 5.8              2.7          5.1          1.9     virginica
```

5.4 Quiz Questions

1 Ranuni gives the _____ distribution of the random variables in Seed.
   A Normal
   B Uniform
   C Chi-Square
   D Gamma

2 Which of the following statements is used for categorical variables?
   A VAR
   B CONTENTS
   C SORT
   D CLASS

3 The use of ALL statement in proc tabulate sums all the rows under a new variable.
   A True
   B False

4 _____ procedure can also output two tables simultaneously for different variables.
   A Proc Contents
   B Proc Freq
   C Proc Means
   D Proc Tabulate

5 In Proc Means, to get the 25th percentile of a variable, the statistic is:
   A Percentile25
   B 25percentile
   C P25
   D 25P

6 Fread function is in which package of R?
   A dplyr
   B data.table
   C ggplot2
   D hmisc

7 Function Object.size:
   A All data.tables in memory, columns, and their keys.
   B Collects information about current R session.
   C Provides memory used to store an R object.
   D Reads in data in the fastest manner.

8 Arrange sorts the data in ascending order according to the variable specified.
   A True
   B False

9 Which of the following function removes all the existing variables preserving only the new one?
   A Mutate
   B Transmute
   C Select
   D Groupby

10 Random n rows are selected in a table using:
    A nrow
    B ncol
    C sample()
    D sample_n()

Quiz Answers

1 B. Uniform

2 D. CLASS

3 A. True

4 D. Proc Tabulate

5 C. P25

6 B. data.table

7 C. Provides memory used to store an R object.

8 A. True

9 B. Transmute

10 D. sample_n()

6

Frequency Distributions and Cross Tabulations

We have used numeric summary methods in the previous chapter to see analysis of numerical variables. In this chapter we learn how to use frequency distributions and cross tabulations to analyze categorical or factor variables.

6.1   Frequency Distributions in SAS

Proc Freq is the primary procedure for frequency analysis.

```
proc freq data=sashelp.cars;
   tables origin;
 run;
```

The FREQ Procedure

Origin	Frequency	Percent	Cumulative Frequency	Cumulative Percent
Asia	158	36.92	158	36.92
Europe	123	28.74	281	65.65
USA	147	34.35	428	100.00

We can use nlevels to find the number of levels in that variable. We can also do frequency analysis on two or more variables by keeping them in tables with a white space between each.

SAS for R Users: A Book for Data Scientists, First Edition. Ajay Ohri.
© 2020 John Wiley & Sons, Inc. Published 2020 by John Wiley & Sons, Inc.

```
proc freq data=sashelp.cars nlevels;
    tables origin type;
  run;
```

The FREQ Procedure

Number of Variable Levels

Variable	Levels
Origin	3
Type	6

Origin	Frequency	Percent	Cumulative Frequency	Cumulative Percent
Asia	158	36.92	158	36.92
Europe	123	28.74	281	65.65
USA	147	34.35	428	100.00

Type	Frequency	Percent	Cumulative Frequency	Cumulative Percent
Hybrid	3	0.70	3	0.70
SUV	60	14.02	63	14.72
Sedan	262	61.21	325	75.93
Sports	49	11.45	374	87.38
Truck	24	5.61	398	92.99
Wagon	30	7.01	428	100.00

We can remove the cumulative frequency, percent, row, col., cumulatives by using the following respectively (**norow, nocol,nopercent,nocum**).

```
proc freq data=sashelp.cars nlevels;
    tables origin type/norow nocol nopercent nocum;
  run;
```

The FREQ Procedure

Number of Variable Levels

Variable	Levels
Origin	3
Type	6

Origin	Frequency
Asia	158
Europe	123
USA	147

Type	Frequency
Hybrid	3
SUV	60
Sedan	262
Sports	49
Truck	24
Wagon	30

We can do a cross tabulation between two variables by simply putting a *
between them in the tables part of proc freq .

```
proc freq data=sashelp.cars nlevels;
   tables origin*type/norow nocol nopercent nocum;
 Run;
```

The FREQ Procedure

Number of Variable Levels

Variable	Levels
Origin	3
Type	6

			Table of Origin by Type				
			Type				
Origin	Hybrid	SUV	Sedan	Sports	Truck	Wagon	Total
Asia	3	25	94	17	8	11	158
Europe	0	10	78	23	0	12	123
USA	0	25	90	9	16	7	147
Total	3	60	262	49	24	30	428

6.2   Frequency Distributions in R

6.2.1   Frequency Tabulations in R

Let's take dataset mtcars in R. We look at help for mtcars using? mtcars
   A data frame with 32 observations on 11 (numeric) variables.

```
[, 1]  mpg   Miles/(US) gallon
[, 2]  cyl   Number of cylinders
[, 3]  disp  Displacement (cu.in.)
[, 4]  hp    Gross horsepower
[, 5]  drat  Rear axle ratio
[, 6]  wt    Weight (1000 lbs)
[, 7]  qsec  1/4 mile time
[, 8]  vs    Engine (0 = V-shaped, 1 = straight)
[, 9]  am    Transmission (0 = automatic, 1 = manual)
[,10]  gear  Number of forward gears
[,11]  carb  Number of carburetors
```

```
> data(mtcars)
> str(mtcars)
'data.frame': 32 obs. of 11 variables:
$ mpg : num 21 21 22.8 21.4 18.7 18.1 14.3 24.4 22.8 19.2 ...
$ cyl : num 6 6 4 6 8 6 8 4 4 6 ...
$ disp: num 160 160 108 258 360 ...
$ hp : num 110 110 93 110 175 105 245 62 95 123 ...
$ drat: num 3.9 3.9 3.85 3.08 3.15 2.76 3.21 3.69 3.92 3.92 ...
$ wt : num 2.62 2.88 2.32 3.21 3.44 ...
$ qsec: num 16.5 17 18.6 19.4 17 ...
$ vs : num 0 0 1 1 0 1 0 1 1 1 ...
$ am : num 1 1 1 0 0 0 0 0 0 0 ...
$ gear: num 4 4 4 3 3 3 3 4 4 4 ...
$ carb: num 4 4 1 1 2 1 4 2 2 4 ...
```

However, the number of cylinders, gears, carburettors and automatic transmission are factor variables as they are discrete not continuous. So, we use as.factor to convert numeric to factor

```
> mtcars$cyl=as.factor(mtcars$cyl)
> mtcars$gear=as.factor(mtcars$gear)
> mtcars$carb=as.factor(mtcars$carb)
> mtcars$am=as.factor(mtcars$am)
> str(mtcars)
'data.frame': 32 obs. of 11 variables:
$ mpg : num 21 21 22.8 21.4 18.7 18.1 14.3 24.4 22.8 19.2 ...
$ cyl : Factor w/ 3 levels "4","6","8": 2 2 1 2 3 2 3 1 1 2 ...
$ disp: num 160 160 108 258 360 ...
$ hp : num 110 110 93 110 175 105 245 62 95 123 ...
$ drat: num 3.9 3.9 3.85 3.08 3.15 2.76 3.21 3.69 3.92 3.92 ...
$ wt : num 2.62 2.88 2.32 3.21 3.44 ...
$ qsec: num 16.5 17 18.6 19.4 17 ...
$ vs : num 0 0 1 1 0 1 0 1 1 1 ...
$ am : Factor w/ 2 levels "0","1": 2 2 2 1 1 1 1 1 1 1 ...
$ gear: Factor w/ 3 levels "3","4","5": 2 2 2 1 1 1 1 2 2 2 ...
$ carb: Factor w/ 6 levels "1","2","3","4",..: 4 4 1 1 2 1 4 2 2 4 ...
```

We now use **table** command just as we used proc freq for frequency and cross tabulation.

```
> table(mtcars$gear)

3    4    5
15   12   5

> table(mtcars$cyl,mtcars$gear)

    3    4   5
4   1    8   2
6   2    4   1
8   12   0   2
```

We can also **xtabs** in R

```
> tt = xtabs(~gear + cyl , data = mtcars)

> ftable(tt)
   cyl  4  6  8
gear
3       1  2 12
4       8  4  0
5       2  1  2
```

We can also use gtables package in R to obtain a familiar SAS-like output table using the **CrossTable** function:

```
> library(gmodels)
> CrossTable(mtcars$gear, mtcars$cyl, max.width=1,expected =
TRUE,prop.r=F,prop.c=F,,prop.t=F,prop.chisq = F)
```

```
Console   Terminal

|----------------------------|
|                       N  |
|            Expected N  |
|----------------------------|


Total Observations in Table:  32

              | mtcars$cyl
 mtcars$gear  |        4  |        6  |        8 | Row Total |
--------------|-----------|-----------|-----------|-----------|
           3  |        1  |        2  |       12 |       15 |
              |    5.156  |    3.281  |    6.562 |          |
--------------|-----------|-----------|-----------|-----------|
           4  |        8  |        4  |        0 |       12 |
              |    4.125  |    2.625  |    5.250 |          |
--------------|-----------|-----------|-----------|-----------|
           5  |        2  |        1  |        2 |        5 |
              |    1.719  |    1.094  |    2.188 |          |
--------------|-----------|-----------|-----------|-----------|
 Column Total |       11  |        7  |       14 |       32 |
--------------|-----------|-----------|-----------|-----------|


Statistics for All Table Factors


Pearson's Chi-squared test
----------------------------------------------------------
Chi^2 =  18.03636     d.f. = 4     p = 0.001214066
```

Figure 6.1 CrossTables output in R.

We can also use **with** function

```
> a1=with(subset(mtcars),table(mtcars$gear,mtcars$cyl))
> a1

      4   6   8
  3   1   2  12
  4   8   4   0
  5   2   1   2
```

6.2.2 Frequency Tabulations in R with Other Variables Statistics

Now let's populate this cross-tabulation with the mean of mileage(mpg)
Using **with**

```
> with(mtcars, tapply(mpg, list(gear,cyl), FUN= mean))
      4      6     8
3 21.500 19.75 15.05
4 26.925 19.75    NA
5 28.200 19.70 15.40
```

Using **reshape2** package and **acast**

```
> library(reshape2)

> acast(mtcars, gear~cyl, value.var='mpg', mean)
      4      6     8
3 21.500 19.75 15.05
4 26.925 19.75   NaN
5 28.200 19.70 15.40
```

Using **xtabs**

```
> xtabs(mpg ~ cyl + gear, mtcars)/table(mtcars[c('cyl', 'gear')])
    gear
cyl  3       4       5
  4 21.500   26.925  28.200
  6 19.750   19.750  19.700
  8 15.050           15.400
```

Using **dcast** from data.table package

```
> library(data.table)
> dcast(as.data.table(mtcars), gear~cyl, value.var='mpg', mean)
   gear    4     6     8
1     3 21.500 19.75 15.05
2     4 26.925 19.75   NaN
3     5 28.200 19.70 15.40
```

Using **spread**

```
library(plyr)
 library(tidyr)
  spread(ddply(mtcars, .(gear, cyl), summarize, new = mean(mpg)),
  gear, new)

   cyl    3     4      5
1    4 21.50  26.925  28.2
2    6 19.75  19.750  19.7
3    8 15.05     NA   15.4
```

This teaches us the following lessons:

- There are many, many ways to do the same thing in R.
- One must find the fastest computational function for the dataset they have.
- An SAS proc has multiple options to create and format output.

6.3   Quiz Questions

1   What is the primary function for frequency analysis in SAS?

2   What is the primary function for frequency analysis in R?

3   For dataset DT how do we do a cross tabulation between Var1 and Var2 in SAS?

4   For dataset DT how do we do a cross tabulation between Var1 and Var2 in R?

5   For Proc Freq how do we remove row statistics in SAS?

6   For CrossTable how do we remove row statistics in R?

7   Which function converts variable to factor variable?

8   What kind of numeric variable is likely to be a factor variable?

9   From data.table package which function is used to get say mean(var3) in a cross table of var 2 and var1?

10   How do we get number of levels in Proc Freq? How is it useful?

Quiz Answers

1   Proc Freq

2   table

3   Proc freq data = DT; tables Var1*Var2;run;

4   Table(DT$Var1,DT$Var2)

5 /norow in the tables line

6 prop.r = F

7 as.factor

8 Discrete values with fewer number of distinct levels.

9 dcast

10 Nlevels, helps to determine number of distinct values that variable has

7

Using SQL with SAS and R

7.1   What is SQL?

SQL (Structured Query Language) is a language for querying and modifying data in Relational Database Management Systems (RDBMs). However SQL is also used within Apache Hive and Python as well as PySpark. The **pandasql** package allows you to query pandas DataFrames using SQL syntax. The entry point into all SQL functionality in Spark is the SQLContext class. The Apache Hive ™ data warehouse software facilitates reading, writing, and managing large datasets residing in distributed storage using SQL.

7.1.1   Basic Terminology

A database is a collection of information that is organized so that it can be easily accessed, managed and updated.

A relational database is a set of tables from which data can be accessed or reassembled in many different ways without having to reorganize the database tables.

7.1.2   CAP Theorem

CAP Theorem is a concept that a distributed database system can only have 2 of the 3: Consistency, Availability, and Partition Tolerance.

- Consistency: Every read receives the most recent write or an error
- Availability: Every request receives a (non-error) response – without the guarantee that it contains the most recent write
- Partition tolerance: The system continues to operate despite an arbitrary number of messages being dropped (or delayed) by the network between nodes.

SAS for R Users: A Book for Data Scientists, First Edition. Ajay Ohri.
© 2020 John Wiley & Sons, Inc. Published 2020 by John Wiley & Sons, Inc.

ACID (Atomicity, Consistency, Isolation, Durability) is a set of properties of database transactions intended to guarantee validity even in the event of errors, power failures, etc.

Eventually-consistent services are sometimes classified as providing BASE (Basically Available, Soft state, Eventual consistency), in contrast to traditional ACID.

Database systems designed with traditional ACID guarantees in mind such as RDBMS choose consistency over availability, whereas systems designed around the BASE philosophy, common in the NoSQL databases, choose availability over consistency.

7.1.3   SQL in SAS and R

SQL can be used in R by the sqldf package and using the sqldf() function whereas in SAS we use PROC SQL for using SQL. Proc sql does not require a run statement because proc sql statements are executed immediately.

7.2   SQL Select

The select statement is used to tell the database what data we want from it.
   The basic syntax of a select statement is:

```
select column1,column2.
from datatable_name
where condition
order by column;
```

We use the * wildcard to select all columns:-

```
select * from datatable.
```

In R:

```
sqldf('select * from mtcars;')
```

We will use the inbuilt mtcars dataset in R and I have also created a mtcars dataset in SAS as follows:

1) Downloaded data from:
   https://vincentarelbundock.github.io/Rdatasets/csv/datasets/mtcars.csv
2) Uploaded to folder in SAS
3) Created a dataset named mtcars using proc import.

```
FILENAME REFFILE '/home/ajay4/sasuser.v94/mtcars.csv';

PROC IMPORT DATAFILE=REFFILE
    DBMS=CSV
    OUT=WORK.mtcars;
    GETNAMES=YES;
RUN;

proc sql number outobs=10;
select * from mtcars;
Run;
```

Row	VAR1	mpg	cyl	disp	hp	drat	wt	qsec	vs	am	gear	carb
1	Mazda RX4	21	6	160	110	3.9	2.62	16.46	0	1	4	4
2	Mazda RX4 Wag	21	6	160	110	3.9	2.875	17.02	0	1	4	4
3	Datsun 710	22.8	4	108	93	3.85	2.32	18.61	1	1	4	1
4	Hornet 4 Drive	21.4	6	258	110	3.08	3.215	19.44	1	0	3	1
5	Hornet Sportabout	18.7	8	360	175	3.15	3.44	17.02	0	0	3	2
6	Valiant	18.1	6	225	105	2.76	3.46	20.22	1	0	3	1
7	Duster 360	14.3	8	360	245	3.21	3.57	15.84	0	0	3	4
8	Merc 240D	24.4	4	146.7	62	3.69	3.19	20	1	0	4	2
9	Merc 230	22.8	4	140.8	95	3.92	3.15	22.9	1	0	4	2
10	Merc 280	19.2	6	167.6	123	3.92	3.44	18.3	1	0	4	4

In SQL * denotes all data.

Using outobs we limit the output to 10.

Using select we select the variables from a particular database satisfying a certain condition (if present). The basic syntax for using sql in SAS is:

```
proc sql outputdata;
select * frominputdata;
```

The syntax for using sql in R is:

```
> install.packages("sqldf")
> library(sqldf)
> sqldf("select * from mtcars limit 10")

    mpg  cyl  disp   hp   drat  wt     qsec   vs  am  gear  carb
1   21.0  6   160.0  110  3.90  2.620  16.46  0   1   4     4
2   21.0  6   160.0  110  3.90  2.875  17.02  0   1   4     4
3   22.8  4   108.0  93   3.85  2.320  18.61  1   1   4     1
4   21.4  6   258.0  110  3.08  3.215  19.44  1   0   3     1
5   18.7  8   360.0  175  3.15  3.440  17.02  0   0   3     2
6   18.1  6   225.0  105  2.76  3.460  20.22  1   0   3     1
7   14.3  8   360.0  245  3.21  3.570  15.84  0   0   3     4
8   24.4  4   146.7  62   3.69  3.190  20.00  1   0   4     2
9   22.8  4   140.8  95   3.92  3.150  22.90  1   0   4     2
10  19.2  6   167.6  123  3.92  3.440  18.30  1   0   4     4
```

Note we used limit to limit the number of rows.

We can select particular columns by specifying their names separated by commas in the select statement:

To select only mpg,vs, and cyl columns:

In R:

```
sqldf('select mpg,vs,cyl from mtcars;')
```

In SAS:

```
proc sql number;
select mpg,vs,cyl from mtcars;
```

7.2.1 SQL WHERE

We use the WHERE clause along with SELECT to conditionally select rows.

For example:
To select only rows which have cyl=6

```
proc sql number;
select * from mtcars where cyl=6;

Proc print data=number;
run;
```

Figure 7.1 Proc SQL in SAS
In R

```
> sqldf("select * from mtcars where cyl=6")

   mpg cyl disp  hp  drat  wt    qsec   vs am gear carb
1 21.0  6  160.0 110 3.90 2.620 16.46  0  1   4    4
2 21.0  6  160.0 110 3.90 2.875 17.02  0  1   4    4
3 21.4  6  258.0 110 3.08 3.215 19.44  1  0   3    1
4 18.1  6  225.0 105 2.76 3.460 20.22  1  0   3    1
5 19.2  6  167.6 123 3.92 3.440 18.30  1  0   4    4
6 17.8  6  167.6 123 3.92 3.440 18.90  1  0   4    4
7 19.7  6  145.0 175 3.62 2.770 15.50  0  1   5    6
Rows which had cyl=6 are selected.
```

7.2.2 SQL Order By

"Order by" is used to display the output sorted. It can be sorted in ascending, descending, or alphabetical order.

In SAS:

```
proc sql number;
select * from mtcars where cyl=6;
order by disp;
run;

Proc print data=number;
run;
```

Row	VAR1	mpg	cyl	disp	hp	drat	wt	qsec	vs	am	gear	carb
1	Mazda RX4	21	6	160	110	3.9	2.62	16.46	0	1	4	4
2	Mazda RX4 Wag	21	6	160	110	3.9	2.875	17.02	0	1	4	4
3	Hornet 4 Drive	21.4	6	258	110	3.08	3.215	19.44	1	0	3	1
4	Valiant	18.1	6	225	105	2.76	3.46	20.22	1	0	3	1
5	Merc 280	19.2	6	167.6	123	3.92	3.44	18.3	1	0	4	4
6	Merc 280C	17.8	6	167.6	123	3.92	3.44	18.9	1	0	4	4
7	Ferrari Dino	19.7	6	145	175	3.62	2.77	15.5	0	1	5	6

Sort/Order Data in SAS

In R

```
> sqldf ("select * from mtcars where cyl=6 order by disp")

    mpg  cyl disp   hp   drat  wt       qsec    vs   am  gear carb
1   19.7  6   145.0  175  3.62  2.770    15.50   0    1   5    6
2   21.0  6   160.0  110  3.90  2.620    16.46   0    1   4    4
3   21.0  6   160.0  110  3.90  2.875    17.02   0    1   4    4
4   19.2  6   167.6  123  3.92  3.440    18.30   1    0   4    4
5   17.8  6   167.6  123  3.92  3.440    18.90   1    0   4    4
6   18.1  6   225.0  105  2.76  3.460    20.22   1    0   3    1
7   21.4  6   258.0  110  3.08  3.215    19.44   1    0   3    1
```

7.2.3   AND, OR, NOT in SQL

AND, OR, and NOT operators can be used along with the WHERE clause.

AND operator displays only those rows which meet all conditions in the WHERE clause.

OR operator displays those rows which meet at least one of the conditions in the WHERE clause.

NOT operator displays those rows which do not meet the condition specified in the WHERE clause.

In SAS:

To select only those rows from mtcars which have cyl=6 as well as gear=3

```
proc sql number1;
select * from mtcars where cyl=6 and gear=3 ;
order by disp;
run;
```

```
Proc print data=number1;
run;

Row VAR1      mpg  cyl disp hp   drat wt     qsec  vs am gear carb
1   Hornet 4 21.4 6   258  110 3.08 3.215 19.44 1  0  3    1
    Drive
2   Valiant  18.1 6   225  105 2.76 3.46  20.22 1  0  3    1
```

To select only those rows which have either carb = 1 or carb = 4

```
proc sql number2;
select * from mtcars where carb=1 or carb=4 ;
order by disp;
run;

Proc print data=number2;
run;
```

Row	VAR1	mpg	cyl	disp	hp	drat	wt	qsec	vs	am	gear	carb
1	Mazda RX4	21	6	160	110	3.9	2.62	16.46	0	1	4	4
2	Mazda RX4 Wag	21	6	160	110	3.9	2.875	17.02	0	1	4	4
3	Datsun 710	22.8	4	108	93	3.85	2.32	18.61	1	1	4	1
4	Hornet 4 Drive	21.4	6	258	110	3.08	3.215	19.44	1	0	3	1
5	Valiant	18.1	6	225	105	2.76	3.46	20.22	1	0	3	1
6	Duster 360	14.3	8	360	245	3.21	3.57	15.84	0	0	3	4
7	Merc 280	19.2	6	167.6	123	3.92	3.44	18.3	1	0	4	4
8	Merc 280C	17.8	6	167.6	123	3.92	3.44	18.9	1	0	4	4
9	Cadillac Fleetwood	10.4	8	472	205	2.93	5.25	17.98	0	0	3	4
10	Lincoln Continental	10.4	8	460	215	3	5.424	17.82	0	0	3	4
11	Chrysler Imperial	14.7	8	440	230	3.23	5.345	17.42	0	0	3	4
12	Fiat 128	32.4	4	78.7	66	4.08	2.2	19.47	1	1	4	1
13	Toyota Corolla	33.9	4	71.1	65	4.22	1.835	19.9	1	1	4	1
14	Toyota Corona	21.5	4	120.1	97	3.7	2.465	20.01	1	0	3	1
15	Camaro Z28	13.3	8	350	245	3.73	3.84	15.41	0	0	3	4
16	Fiat X1-9	27.3	4	79	66	4.08	1.935	18.9	1	1	4	1
17	Ford Pantera L	15.8	8	351	264	4.22	3.17	14.5	0	1	5	4

To select only and all those rows which do not have am=0:

Row	VAR1	mpg	cyl	disp	hp	drat	wt	qsec	vs	am	gear	carb
1	Mazda RX4	21	6	160	110	3.9	2.62	16.46	0	1	4	4
2	Mazda RX4 Wag	21	6	160	110	3.9	2.875	17.02	0	1	4	4
3	Datsun 710	22.8	4	108	93	3.85	2.32	18.61	1	1	4	1
4	Fiat 128	32.4	4	78.7	66	4.08	2.2	19.47	1	1	4	1
5	Honda Civic	30.4	4	75.7	52	4.93	1.615	18.52	1	1	4	2
6	Toyota Corolla	33.9	4	71.1	65	4.22	1.835	19.9	1	1	4	1
7	Fiat X1-9	27.3	4	79	66	4.08	1.935	18.9	1	1	4	1
8	Porsche 914-2	26	4	120.3	91	4.43	2.14	16.7	0	1	5	2
9	Lotus Europa	30.4	4	95.1	113	3.77	1.513	16.9	1	1	5	2
10	Ford Pantera L	15.8	8	351	264	4.22	3.17	14.5	0	1	5	4
11	Ferrari Dino	19.7	6	145	175	3.62	2.77	15.5	0	1	5	6
12	Maserati Bora	15	8	301	335	3.54	3.57	14.6	0	1	5	8
13	Volvo 142E	21.4	4	121	109	4.11	2.78	18.6	1	1	4	2

In R:

To select only those rows from mtcars which have cyl=6 as well as gear=3

```
> sqldf("select * from mtcars where cyl=6 and gear=3 order by
disp")

    mpg  cyl  disp  hp   drat  wt     qsec   vs  am  gear  carb
1   18.1 6    225   105  2.76  3.460  20.22  1   0   3     1
2   21.4 6    258   110  3.08  3.215  19.44  1   0   3     1
```

To select only those rows which have either carb=1 or carb=4

```
> sqldf("select * from mtcars where carb=1 or carb=4 order by
disp")

    mpg  cyl  disp  hp   drat  wt     qsec   vs  am  gear  carb
1   33.9 4    71.1  65   4.22  1.835  19.90  1   1   4     1
2   32.4 4    78.7  66   4.08  2.200  19.47  1   1   4     1
```

3	27.3	4	79.0	66	4.08	1.935	18.90	1	1	4	1
4	22.8	4	108.0	93	3.85	2.320	18.61	1	1	4	1
5	21.5	4	120.1	97	3.70	2.465	20.01	1	0	3	1
6	21.0	6	160.0	110	3.90	2.620	16.46	0	1	4	4
7	21.0	6	160.0	110	3.90	2.875	17.02	0	1	4	4
8	19.2	6	167.6	123	3.92	3.440	18.30	1	0	4	4
9	17.8	6	167.6	123	3.92	3.440	18.90	1	0	4	4
10	18.1	6	225.0	105	2.76	3.460	20.22	1	0	3	1
11	21.4	6	258.0	110	3.08	3.215	19.44	1	0	3	1
12	13.3	8	350.0	245	3.73	3.840	15.41	0	0	3	4
13	15.8	8	351.0	264	4.22	3.170	14.50	0	1	5	4
14	14.3	8	360.0	245	3.21	3.570	15.84	0	0	3	4
15	14.7	8	440.0	230	3.23	5.345	17.42	0	0	3	4
16	10.4	8	460.0	215	3.00	5.424	17.82	0	0	3	4
17	10.4	8	472.0	205	2.93	5.250	17.98	0	0	3	4

To select only and all those rows which do not have am=0

```
> sqldf("select * from mtcars where not am=0 order by disp")

     mpg  cyl disp  hp   drat  wt     qsec   vs  am  gear carb
1    33.9  4  71.1  65   4.22  1.835  19.90  1   1   4    1
2    30.4  4  75.7  52   4.93  1.615  18.52  1   1   4    2
3    32.4  4  78.7  66   4.08  2.200  19.47  1   1   4    1
4    27.3  4  79.0  66   4.08  1.935  18.90  1   1   4    1
5    30.4  4  95.1  113  3.77  1.513  16.90  1   1   5    2
6    22.8  4  108.0 93   3.85  2.320  18.61  1   1   4    1
7    26.0  4  120.3 91   4.43  2.140  16.70  0   1   5    2
8    21.4  4  121.0 109  4.11  2.780  18.60  1   1   4    2
9    19.7  6  145.0 175  3.62  2.770  15.50  0   1   5    6
10   21.0  6  160.0 110  3.90  2.620  16.46  0   1   4    4
11   21.0  6  160.0 110  3.90  2.875  17.02  0   1   4    4
12   15.0  8  301.0 335  3.54  3.570  14.60  0   1   5    8
13   15.8  8  351.0 264  4.22  3.170  14.50  0   1   5    4
```

7.2.4 SQL Select Distinct

We can select only the unique values of a column using the SELECT DISTINCT statement:

For example:

To know what the distinct values are that the variable gear takes in mtcars:-

In SAS:

```
proc sql number;
select distinct gear from mtcars;

Row      gear
1        3
2        4
3        5
```

In R

```
> sqldf ("select distinct gear from mtcars")
gear
1  4
2  3
3  5
```

7.2.5   SQL INSERT INTO

INSERT INTO statement is used to add rows to a data table.

- While using statements like INSERT INTO, ALTER TABLE, UPDATE which make changes to a data table in R, it is important to remember that sqldf() makes a copy of the data table provided to it, makes the required changes and returns the copy with the required changes.
- To make changes on the original data table, we need to assign the copy of the table returned by sqldf() to the object that stored the original copy.
- To use multiple SQL statements in sqldf(), we use the c() function.
- Proc Sql on the other hand makes the changes on the original copy itself.

To Insert a Row in SAS:

Note Var1 has taken the value of row.names from input R dataset.

To delete existing dataset we use Proc Delete

```
proc delete data=mtcars;
run;
```

FILENAME REFFILE '/home/ajay4/sasuser.v94/mtcars.csv';

```
PROC IMPORT DATAFILE=REFFILE
    DBMS=CSV
    OUT=WORK.mtcars;
    GETNAMES=YES;

RUN;

proc sql;
insert into mtcars values('Maserati Bora',19.0,6,315.0,355,3.84,3.170,14.55,1,0,4,2) ;
select * from mtcars;run;

proc print data=mtcars (firstobs=27 obs=33) ;run;
```

Obs	VAR1	mpg	cyl	disp	hp	drat	wt	qsec	vs	am	gear	carb
27	Porsche 914-2	26	4	120.3	91	4.43	2.14	16.7	0	1	5	2
28	Lotus Europa	30.4	4	95.1	113	3.77	1.513	16.9	1	1	5	2
29	Ford Pantera	L15.8	8	351	264	4.22	3.17	14.5	0	1	5	4
30	Ferrari Dino	19.7	6	145	175	3.62	2.77	15.5	0	1	5	6
31	Maserati Bora	15	8	301	335	3.54	3.57	14.6	0	1	5	8
32	Volvo 142E	21.4	4	121	109	4.11	2.78	18.6	1	1	4	2
33	Maserati Bora	19	6	315	355	3.84	3.17	14.55	1	0	4	2

To insert a row in mtcars in R:

```
data(mtcars)

mtcars=sqldf(c("insert into mtcars values(19.0,6,315.0,355,3.84,
3.170,14.55,1,0,4,2)","select * from mtcars"))

tail(mtcars)

      mpg   cyl  disp   hp    drat   wt     qsec    vs   am   gear  carb
28    30.4  4    95.1   113   3.77   1.513  16.90   1    1    5     2
29    15.8  8    351.0  264   4.22   3.170  14.50   0    1    5     4
30    19.7  6    145.0  175   3.62   2.770  15.50   0    1    5     6
31    15.0  8    301.0  335   3.54   3.570  14.60   0    1    5     8
32    21.4  4    121.0  109   4.11   2.780  18.60   1    1    4     2
33    19.0  6    315.0  355   3.84   3.170  14.55   1    0    4     2
```

Note the use of c() function and that we have assigned the result of sqldf ()
to mtcars. Also note the output has 33 rows instead of the initial 32 with the
new row having the input values.

7.2.6   SQL Delete

The DELETE statement is used along with WHERE to conditionally delete rows.

In SAS:

```
proc sql ;
delete from mtcars
where gear=3 or cyl=4;
select * from mtcars;

proc print data=mtcars;
run;
```

Obs	VAR1	mpg	cyl	disp	hp	drat	wt	qsec	vs	am	gear	carb
1	Mazda RX4	21	6	160	110	3.9	2.62	16.46	0	1	4	4
2	Mazda RX4 Wag	21	6	160	110	3.9	2.875	17.02	0	1	4	4
10	Merc 280	19.2	6	167.6	123	3.92	3.44	18.3	1	0	4	4
11	Merc 280C	17.8	6	167.6	123	3.92	3.44	18.9	1	0	4	4
29	Ford Pantera L	15.8	8	351	264	4.22	3.17	14.5	0	1	5	4
30	Ferrari Dino	19.7	6	145	175	3.62	2.77	15.5	0	1	5	6
31	Maserati Bora	15	8	301	335	3.54	3.57	14.6	0	1	5	8

In R:

```
data(mtcars)
mtcars2=sqldf(c("delete from mtcars where gear=3 or
cyl=4","select * from mtcars"))
mtcars2

> mtcars2
    mpg  cyl disp    hp   drat   wt     qsec    vs   am   gear carb
1   21.0  6   160.0  110  3.90   2.620  16.46   0    1    4    4
2   21.0  6   160.0  110  3.90   2.875  17.02   0    1    4    4
3   19.2  6   167.6  123  3.92   3.440  18.30   1    0    4    4
4   17.8  6   167.6  123  3.92   3.440  18.90   1    0    4    4
5   15.8  8   351.0  264  4.22   3.170  14.50   0    1    5    4
6   19.7  6   145.0  175  3.62   2.770  15.50   0    1    5    6
7   15.0  8   301.0  335  3.54   3.570  14.60   0    1    5    8
```

7.2.7 SQL Aggregate Functions

Aggregate functions perform a calculation on a set of values and return a single value. Some aggregate functions are min(),max(),avg.(),sum(),count() are:

Aggregate functions ignore missing values except count().

- min() gives the minimum value of the column.
- max() gives the maximum value of the column.
- avg.() gives the average value of the values in the column.
- sum() gives the sum of all values in the column.
- count() gives the number of non missing values in a column.

In SAS:

```
Here we replace earlier values of MTCARS by replace option in
proc import

FILENAME REFFILE '/home/ajay4/sasuser.v94/mtcars.csv';

PROC IMPORT DATAFILE=REFFILE replace
     DBMS=CSV
     OUT=WORK.mtcars;
     GETNAMES=YES;
RUN;
```

```
proc sql;
Create table mtcars2 as
select min(mpg), max(mpg),avg(mpg) from mtcars;
Run;

Proc print data=mtcars2;
Run;
```

Obs	_TEMG001	_TEMG002	_TEMG003
1	10.4	33.9	20.0906

Here, **create table** creates a new table mtcars2

In R:

```
> sqldf("select min(mpg),max(mpg),avg(mpg) from mtcars")

     min(mpg)      max(mpg)       avg(mpg)
1     10.4          33.9         20.09062
```

7.2.8 SQL ALIASES

Aliases are used to give a temporary name. The AS clause is used with SELECT to do so.

In SAS:

```
proc sql;
Create table mtcars2 as
select min(mpg) as minimum, max(mpg) as maximum, avg(mpg) as
average from import;
Run;

Proc print data=mtcars2;
Run;

Obs      minimum        maximum          average
1        10.4           33.9           20.0906
```

In R:

```
> sqldf("select min(mpg) AS minimum from mtcars;")
  minimum
1    10.4
```

7.2.9 SQL ALTER TABLE

ALTER TABLE is used to add, delete or modify column names in SAS. ADD,DELETE,MODIFY are clauses that can be used with ALTER TABLE. The new column added contains null values by default.

```
ALTER TABLE dataset ADD column_name column_type
```

To make a new column in mtcars with the label 'name' and of type char.

In SAS:

```
proc sql;
alter table mtcars add name char;
Run;
```

Variables in Creation Order					
#	Variable	Type	Len	Format	Informat
1	VAR1	Char	21	$21.	$21.
2	mpg	Num	8	BEST12.	BEST32.
3	cyl	Num	8	BEST12.	BEST32.
4	disp	Num	8	BEST12.	BEST32.
5	hp	Num	8	BEST12.	BEST32.
6	drat	Num	8	BEST12.	BEST32.
7	wt	Num	8	BEST12.	BEST32.
8	qsec	Num	8	BEST12.	BEST32.
9	vs	Num	8	BEST12.	BEST32.
10	am	Num	8	BEST12.	BEST32.
11	gear	Num	8	BEST12.	BEST32.
12	carb	Num	8	BEST12.	BEST32.
13	name	Char	8		

In R:

```
mtcars3=sqldf(c("alter table mtcars add name char","select *
from mtcars"))
head(mtcars3)

    mpg  cyl disp hp    drat  wt      qsec    vs am gear carb name
1  21.0  6   160  110  3.90  2.620  16.46  0  1   4    4    <NA>
2  21.0  6   160  110  3.90  2.875  17.02  0  1   4    4    <NA>
3  22.8  4   108  93   3.85  2.320  18.61  1  1   4    1    <NA>
4  21.4  6   258  110  3.08  3.215  19.44  1  0   3    1    <NA>
5  18.7  8   360  175  3.15  3.440  17.02  0  0   3    2    <NA>
6  18.1  6   225  105  2.76  3.460  20.22  1  0   3    1    <NA>

str(mtcars3)
> str(mtcars3)
'data.frame':  32 obs. of 12 variables:
 $ mpg : num 21 21 22.8 21.4 18.7 18.1 14.3 24.4 22.8 19.2 ...
 $ cyl : num 6 6 4 6 8 6 8 4 4 6 ...
 $ disp: num 160 160 108 258 360 ...
 $ hp  : num 110 110 93 110 175 105 245 62 95 123 ...
 $ drat: num 3.9 3.9 3.85 3.08 3.15 2.76 3.21 3.69 3.92 3.92 ...
 $ wt  : num 2.62 2.88 2.32 3.21 3.44 ...
 $ qsec: num 16.5 17 18.6 19.4 17 ...
 $ vs  : num 0 0 1 1 0 1 0 1 1 1 ...
 $ am  : num 1 1 1 0 0 0 0 0 0 0 ...
 $ gear: num 4 4 4 3 3 3 3 4 4 4 ...
 $ carb: num 4 4 1 1 2 1 4 2 2 4 ...
 $ name: chr NA NA NA NA ...
```

7.2.10   SQL UPDATE

UPDATE is used to make changes to the rows of a table and is used with the SET and WHERE clause.

In SAS:

```
Data mtcars;
Set import;
run;

proc sql;
alter table mtcars add name char;
Run;
```

```
proc sql;
alter table mtcars add name char;
Run;

proc sql ;
update mtcars set name="Economy" where cyl=4;

proc sql ;
update mtcars set name="Luxury" where cyl=6;

proc sql ;
update mtcars set name="Muscle" where cyl=8;
```

Obs	VAR1	mpg	cyl	disp	hp	drat	wt	qsec	vs	am	gear	carb	name
1	Mazda RX4	21	6	160	110	3.9	2.62	16.46	0	1	4	4	'Luxury'
2	Mazda RX4 Wag	21	6	160	110	3.9	2.875	17.02	0	1	4	4	'Luxury'
3	Datsun 710	22.8	4	108	93	3.85	2.32	18.61	1	1	4	1	'Economy'
4	Hornet 4 Drive	21.4	6	258	110	3.08	3.215	19.44	1	0	3	1	'Luxury'
5	Hornet Sportabout	18.7	8	360	175	3.15	3.44	17.02	0	0	3	2	'Muscle'
6	Valiant	18.1	6	225	105	2.76	3.46	20.22	1	0	3	1	'Luxury'
7	Duster 360	14.3	8	360	245	3.21	3.57	15.84	0	0	3	4	'Muscle'
8	Merc 240D	24.4	4	146.7	62	3.69	3.19	20	1	0	4	2	'Economy'
9	Merc 230	22.8	4	140.8	95	3.92	3.15	22.9	1	0	4	2	'Economy'
10	Merc 280	19.2	6	167.6	123	3.92	3.44	18.3	1	0	4	4	'Luxury'

In R:

```
mtcars=sqldf(c("alter table mtcars add name char","select * from
mtcars"))

mtcars=sqldf(c("update mtcars set name ='Economy' where
cyl=4","select * from mtcars"))
mtcars=sqldf(c("update mtcars set name ='Luxury' where
cyl=6","select * from mtcars"))
mtcars=sqldf(c("update mtcars set name ='Muscle' where
cyl=8","select * from mtcars"))
head(mtcars)

> head(mtcars)
```

```
     mpg  cyl disp  hp   drat  wt    qsec   vs  am  gear carb name
1   21.0  6   160  110  3.90  2.620 16.46  0   1    4    4    Luxury
2   21.0  6   160  110  3.90  2.875 17.02  0   1    4    4    Luxury
3   22.8  4   108  93   3.85  2.320 18.61  1   1    4    1    Economy
4   21.4  6   258  110  3.08  3.215 19.44  1   0    3    1    Luxury
5   18.7  8   360  175  3.15  3.440 17.02  0   0    3    2    Muscle
6   18.1  6   225  105  2.76  3.460 20.22  1   0    3    1    Luxury
```

7.2.11 SQL IS NULL

Missing values in SQL are checked by IS NULL or IS NOT NULL. We take the airquality dataset from https://vincentarelbundock.github.io/Rdatasets/csv/datasets/airquality.csv

Example:
To select all rows with missing values in the Ozone column:of airquality:

In SAS (first we replace NA missing value of R with missing value in SAS using compress. We use outobs in Proc SQL to limit output to five rows.

```
data import2;
set import2 ;
Ozone=compress(Ozone,"NA","");
Run;

proc sql outobs=5 ;
select * from import2 where Ozone IS NULL;

VAR1       Ozone       SolarR      Wind      Temp      Month      Day
5                      NA          14.3      56        5          5
10                     194         8.6       69        5          10
25                     66          16.6      57        5          25
26                     266         14.9      58        5          26
27                     NA          8         57        5          27
```

In R:

```
> sqldf("select * from airquality where Ozone IS NULL LIMIT 5")

      Ozone      Solar.R      Wind      Temp      Month      Day
1     NA         NA           14.3      56        5          5
2     NA         194          8.6       69        5          10
3     NA         66           16.6      57        5          25
4     NA         266          14.9      58        5          26
5     NA         NA           8.0       57        5          27

We chose top 5 rows using LIMIT 5 for printing purposes
```

7.2.12   SQL LIKE and BETWEEN

The LIKE option is used along with WHERE and wildcards like % and _ to select rows that have values with a specified pattern in a column:

- % is used to denote a string of characters
- _ is used to denote a single character.

In SAS:

```
proc sql outobs=5;
select * from mtcars where name like 'L%' ;
```

VAR1	mpg	cyl	disp	hp	drat	wt	qsec	vs	am	gear	carb	name
Mazda RX4	21	6	160	110	3.9	2.62	16.46	0	1	4	4	Luxury
Mazda RX4 Wag	21	6	160	110	3.9	2.875	17.02	0	1	4	4	Luxury
Hornet 4 Drive	21.4	6	258	110	3.08	3.215	19.44	1	0	3	1	Luxury
Valiant	18.1	6	225	105	2.76	3.46	20.22	1	0	3	1	Luxury
Merc 280	19.2	6	167.6	123	3.92	3.44	18.3	1	0	4	4	Luxury

```
proc sql outobs=5 ;
select * from mtcars where name not like 'L%' ;
```

VAR1	mpg	cyl	disp	hp	drat	wt	qsec	vs	am	gear	carb	name
Datsun 710	22.8	4	108	93	3.85	2.32	18.61	1	1	4	1	Economy
Hornet Sportabout	18.7	8	360	175	3.15	3.44	17.02	0	0	3	2	Muscle
Duster 360	14.3	8	360	245	3.21	3.57	15.84	0	0	3	4	Muscle
Merc 240D	24.4	4	146.7	62	3.69	3.19	20	1	0	4	2	Economy
Merc 230	22.8	4	140.8	95	3.92	3.15	22.9	1	0	4	2	Economy

In R:

```
> sqldf("select * from mtcars where name like 'L%' LIMIT 5;")

    mpg cyl disp  hp drat   wt   qsec vs am gear carb name
1 21.0  6 160.0 110 3.90 2.620 16.46  0  1    4    4 Luxury
2 21.0  6 160.0 110 3.90 2.875 17.02  0  1    4    4 Luxury
3 21.4  6 258.0 110 3.08 3.215 19.44  1  0    3    1 Luxury
4 18.1  6 225.0 105 2.76 3.460 20.22  1  0    3    1 Luxury
5 19.2  6 167.6 123 3.92 3.440 18.30  1  0    4    4 Luxury
```

BETWEEN operator can also be used with WHERE as follows:

```
> sqldf("select * from mtcars where mpg between 10 and 14;")

    mpg cyl disp hp  drat wt     qsec  vs am gear carb name
1  10.4 8   472  205 2.93 5.250  17.98 0  0  3    4    Muscle
2  10.4 8   460  215 3.00 5.424  17.82 0  0  3    4    Muscle
3  13.3 8   350  245 3.73 3.840  15.41 0  0  3    4    Muscle
```

7.2.13 SQL GROUP BY

The GROUP BY statement is used with aggregate functions to calculate the corresponding values separately for all groups of a column. It is similar to the CLASS operator in PROC MEANS and group by operator in Hmisc in R and in data table. For multiple variables in R, we use llist in Hmisc::summarize and .(var1,var2) in data.table.

To calculate the average of mpg for each of the distinct values that cyl can take:

In SAS:

```
proc sql;
select avg(mpg) as Avg_mpg ,cyl from mtcars group by cyl;

Avg_mpg     cyl
26.66364    4
19.74286    6
15.1        8

proc sql;
select avg(mpg) as Avg_mpg,cyl,gear from mtcars group by
cyl,gear ;

Avg_mpg     cyl     gear
21.5        4       3
26.925      4       4
28.2        4       5
19.75       6       3
19.75       6       4
19.7        6       5
15.05       8       3
15.4        8       5
```

In R:

```
> sqldf("select avg(mpg),cyl from mtcars group by cyl ;")

     avg(mpg)     cyl
1    26.66364     4
2    19.74286     6
3    15.10000     8

> sqldf("select avg(mpg),cyl,gear from mtcars group by
cyl,gear ;")

     avg(mpg)     cyl      gear
1    21.500       4        3
2    26.925       4        4
3    28.200       4        5
4    19.750       6        3
5    19.750       6        4
6    19.700       6        5
7    15.050       8        3
8    15.400       8        5
```

7.2.14   SQL HAVING

SQL HAVING

HAVING is used after GROUP BY to select only certain groups from the grouped aggregate values.

To display only those values of avg(mpg) grouped by cyl which have avg(mpg) >19 and sorted in ascending order of avg(mpg).

In SAS:

```
proc sql number ;
select cyl,avg(mpg) as avg_mpg from mtcars group by cyl having
avg(mpg)>19 order by avg_mpg;

Row    cyl     avg_mpg
1      6       19.74286
2      4       26.66364
```

In R:

```
> sqldf ("select avg(mpg),cyl from mtcars group by cyl having
avg(mpg)>19 order by avg(mpg);")

    avg(mpg)    cyl
1   19.74286    6
2   26.66364    4

> sqldf ("select avg(mpg),cyl from mtcars group by cyl,gear
having avg(mpg)>19 order by avg(mpg);")

    avg(mpg)    cyl
1   19.700      6
2   19.750      6
3   19.750      6
4   21.500      4
5   26.925      4
6   28.200      4
```

7.2.15   SQL CREATE TABLE and SQL CONSTRAINTS

CREATE TABLE clause can be used to create a table in SQL. NOT NULL and
UNIQUE are CONSTRAINTS in SQL. They are used in front of the variable to
specify that values in the user_id column cannot be missing and cannot be
repeated respectively.

In SAS:

```
proc sql;
create table user(
  user_id integer not null unique ,
  name character,
  age integer)
  ;

proc sql;
insert into user values(1,'John',19);
insert into user values(2,'Sarah',20);
insert into user values(3,'Jack',21) ;

proc print data=user;run;
```

Obs	user_id	Name	Age
1	1	John	19
2	2	Sarah	20
3	3	Jack	21

```
proc sql;
create table book(
book_id integer not null unique,
book_name character,
book_author character
);

proc sql;
insert into book values (1,'Inferno', 'Dan Brown');
insert into book values (2,'Deception Point', 'Dan Brown');
insert into book values (3,'Witches','Roald Dahl');
insert into book values (4,'Hunger Games','Suzanne Collins') ;

proc sql;
alter table user
add primary key (book_id);

proc print data=book;run;
```

Obs	book_id	book_name	book_author
1	1	Inferno	Dan Brow
2	2	Deceptio	Dan Brow
3	3	Witches	Roald Da
4	4	Hunger G	Suzanne

Proc SQL in SAS.

Note: The string values have been truncated in proc sql.

In R:

```
book=sqldf(c("insert into book values(1,'Inferno', 'Dan Brown'),
            (2,'Deception Point','Dan Brown'),
            (3,'Witches','Roald Dahl'),
            (4,'Hunger Games','Suzanne Collins') ","select*from book"))
```

Figure 7.2 Sort/Order Data in SAS.

book

```
##    book_id         book_name        book_author
## 1        1           Inferno          Dan Brown
## 2        2 Deception Point          Dan Brown
## 3        3           Witches        Roald Dahl
## 4        4   Hunger Games Suzanne Collins
```

Figure 7.3 Proc SQL – Create and Insert in SAS.

There is only one INSERT INTO statement is used in R and data values for multiple rows are separated by commas whereas the number of INSERT INTO statements needed in SAS equals the number of rows to be inserted.

PRIMARY KEY is another constraint in SQL which is used to uniquely identify a row in a table.

Columns with only the UNIQUE constraint can have null values whereas PRIMARY KEY columns cannot have null values. There can be several columns with UNIQUE constraint in a data table whereas there can be only one PRIMARY KEY column in a data table.

7.2.16   SQL UNION

UNION clause with select is used to select all observations which lie in at least one of the result sets. UNION ALL can be used to select the observations that lie in both the result sets twice along with the observations that lie in only one of them.

To select all observations which have either cyl=6 or gear=4 or both

In SAS:

```
proc sql number;
select * from mtcars where cyl=6 union select * from mtcars
where gear=4;
```

Row	mpg	cyl	disp	hp	drat	wt	qsec	vs	am	gear	carb	name
1	17.8	6	167.6	123	3.92	3.44	18.9	1	0	4	4	merc
2	18.1	6	225	105	2.76	3.46	20.22	1	0	3	1	merc
3	19.2	6	167.6	123	3.92	3.44	18.3	1	0	4	4	merc
4	21	6	160	110	3.9	2.62	16.46	0	1	4	4	merc
5	21	6	160	110	3.9	2.875	17.02	0	1	4	4	merc
6	22.4	4	121	109	4.11	2.78	18.6	1	1	4	2	limo
7	22.4	6	258	110	3.08	3.215	19.44	1	0	3	1	merc
8	22.8	4	108	93	3.85	2.32	18.61	1	1	4	1	limo
9	22.8	4	140.8	95	3.92	3.15	22.9	1	0	4	2	limo
10	24.4	4	146.7	62	3.69	3.19	20	1	0	4	2	limo
11	27.3	4	79	66	4.08	1.935	18.9	1	1	4	1	limo
12	30.4	4	75.7	52	4.93	1.615	18.52	1	1	4	2	limo
13	32.4	4	78.7	66	4.08	2.2	19.47	1	1	4	1	limo
14	33.9	4	71.1	65	4.22	1.835	19.9	1	1	4	1	limo

Figure 7.4 Proc SQL – Where Condition Result in SAS.

In R:

```
sqldf("select * from mtcars where cyl=6 union select * from mtcars where gear=4")

##      mpg cyl  disp  hp drat    wt  qsec vs am gear carb name
## 1  17.8   6 167.6 123 3.92 3.440 18.90  1  0    4    4 merc
## 2  18.1   6 225.0 105 2.76 3.460 20.22  1  0    3    1 merc
## 3  19.2   6 167.6 123 3.92 3.440 18.30  1  0    4    4 merc
## 4  21.0   6 160.0 110 3.90 2.620 16.46  0  1    4    4 merc
## 5  21.0   6 160.0 110 3.90 2.875 17.02  0  1    4    4 merc
## 6  22.4   4 121.0 109 4.11 2.780 18.60  1  1    4    2 limo
## 7  22.4   6 258.0 110 3.08 3.215 19.44  1  0    3    1 merc
## 8  22.8   4 108.0  93 3.85 2.320 18.61  1  1    4    1 limo
## 9  22.8   4 140.8  95 3.92 3.150 22.90  1  0    4    2 limo
## 10 24.4   4 146.7  62 3.69 3.190 20.00  1  0    4    2 limo
## 11 27.3   4  79.0  66 4.08 1.935 18.90  1  1    4    1 limo
## 12 30.4   4  75.7  52 4.93 1.615 18.52  1  1    4    2 limo
## 13 32.4   4  78.7  66 4.08 2.200 19.47  1  1    4    1 limo
## 14 33.9   4  71.1  65 4.22 1.835 19.90  1  1    4    1 limo
```

Figure 7.5 sqldf – Where Condition in R.

7.2.17   SQL JOINS

SQL JOINS can be used to merge data from more than one table into a single table.

INNER JOIN
Inner Join is used to select only those records that have the same value for a particular column.

LEFT JOIN
Left Join is used to select all records from the first table and those records from the second table which have common values in both tables for the specified column.

Let's take these tables -issued, book and user.

Figure 7.6 Issued table.

```
issued

##    issue_id user_id book_id
## 1         1       2       1
## 2         2       2       3
## 3         3       3       4
```

And book table.

Figure 7.7
Book table.

```
book

##    book_id      book_name      book_author
## 1        1         Inferno        Dan Brown
## 2        2 Deception Point        Dan Brown
## 3        3         Witches      Roald Dahl
## 4        4   Hunger Games  Suzanne Collins
```

And
User

Obs	user_id	name	age
1	1	John	19
2	2	Sarah	20
3	3	Jack	21

Figure 7.8 User table.

In SAS – Inner Join:

```
proc sql;
select * from issued inner join user on issued.user_id=user.
user_id;
```

Figure 7.9 Inner Join in SAS.

issue_id	user_id	book_id	user_id	name	age
1	2	1	2	Sarah	20
2	2	3	2	Sarah	20
3	3	4	3	Jack	21

```
sqldf("select * from issued inner join user on issued.user_id=user.user_id")

##   issue_id user_id book_id user_id..4  name age
## 1        1       2       1          2 Sarah  20
## 2        2       2       3          2 Sarah  20
## 3        3       3       4          3  Jack  21
```

Figure 7.10 Inner Join in R.

In SAS – Left Join:

```
proc sql;
select * from user left join issued on issued.user_id=user.
user_id;
```

Figure 7.11 Left Join in SAS.

user_id	name	age	issue_id	user_id	book_id
1	John	19	.	.	.
2	Sarah	20	1	2	1
2	Sarah	20	2	2	3
3	Jack	21	3	3	4

In R:

```
sqldf("select * from user left join issued on issued.user_id=user.user_id")

##   user_id  name age issue_id user_id..5 book_id
## 1       1  John  19       NA         NA      NA
## 2       2 Sarah  20        1          2       1
## 3       2 Sarah  20        2          2       3
## 4       3  Jack  21        3          3       4
```

Figure 7.12 Left Join in R.

There are many types of JOINs in SQL:

- Inner Join:
- Full Outer Join:
- Left Outer Join:
- Right Outer Join:
- Self-Join:
- Cross Join:

7.3 Merges

We use the merge function in both SAS and R and compare them with the SQL Joins. First, we make the tables in SAS and export the data to import it in R.

```
proc sql;
create table book(
book_id integer not null unique,
book_name character,
book_author character
);

proc sql;
insert into book values(1,'Inferno', 'Dan Brown');
insert into book values(2,'Deception Point','Dan Brown');
insert into book values (3,'Witches','Roald Dahl');
insert into book values (4,'Hunger Games','Suzanne Collins') ;

proc sql;
alter table user
add primary key (book_id);
proc print data=book;run;

proc sql;
create table user(
 user_id integer not null unique ,
 name character,
 age integer)
 ;

proc sql;
insert into user values(1,'John',19);
insert into user values(2,'Sarah',20);
insert into user values(3,'Jack',21) ;
proc print data=user;run;
```

```
proc sql;
create table issued(
issue_id integer not null unique,
user_id integer ,
 book_id integer
);

proc sql;
insert into issued values(1,2, 1);
insert into issued values(2,2,3);
insert into issued values (3,3,4);

proc sql;
alter table issued
add primary key (issue_id );

proc print data=issued ;run;
```

Obs	book_id	book_name	book_author
1	1	Inferno	Dan Brow
2	2	Deceptio	Dan Brow
3	3	Witches	Roald Da
4	4	Hunger G	Suzanne

Obs	user_id	name	age
1	1	John	19
2	2	Sarah	20
3	3	Jack	21

Obs	issue_id	user_id	book_id
1	1	2	1
2	2	2	3
3	3	3	4

We first use the libname statement to make the datasets permanent.

```
libname book '/home/ajay4/book' ;
run;


data book.issued;
set issued;
run;


data book.user;
set issued;
run;


data book.book;
set issued;
Run;


We merge using the following


proc sort data=issued;
by user_id;
run;


proc sort data=user;
by user_id;
run;


data issueduser;
merge issued(in=a) user(in=b);
by user_id;
run;


proc print data=issueduser;
Run;

Obs      issue_id       user_id       book_id       name       age
1           .              1             .           John        19
2           1              2             1           Sarah       20
3           2              2             3           Sarah       20
4           3              3             4           Jack        21
```

Let's try a left join

```
data issueduser;
merge issued(in=a) user(in=b);
by user_id;
run;

proc print data=issueduser;
Run;
```

Obs	issue_id	user_id	book_id	name	age
1	1	2	1	Sarah	20
2	2	2	3	Sarah	20
3	3	3	4	Jack	21

We download the datasets using the download button.

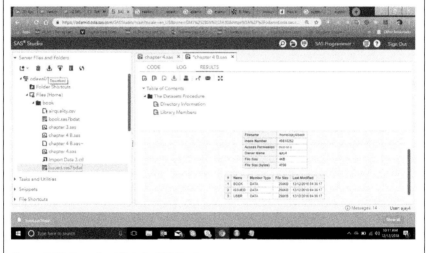

Figure 7.13 Download Data in SAS Studio.

We then read them in R using the following:

```
> install.packages("sas7bdat")
> library("sas7bdat", lib.loc="~/R/win-library/3.5")
 setwd('C:\\Users\\ajay\\Music')
 dir()
 book=read.sas7bdat('book.sas7bdat')
 issued=read.sas7bdat('issued.sas7bdat')
 user=read.sas7bdat('user.sas7bdat')
```

```
> setwd('C:\\Users\\ajayohri\\Music')

> dir()
[1] "book.csv" "book.sas7bdat" "desktop.ini" "issued.sas7bdat"
[5] "user.sas7bdat" "Videos - Shortcut.lnk"

> book=read.sas7bdat('book.sas7bdat')
> issued=read.sas7bdat('issued.sas7bdat')
> user=read.sas7bdat('user.sas7bdat')

> book
  book_id book_name book_author
1 1       Inferno   Dan Brow
2 2       Deceptio  Dan Brow
3 3       Witches   Roald Da
4 4       Hunger G  Suzanne

> issued
  issue_id user_id book_id
1 1        2       1
2 2        2       3
3 3        3       4

> user
  user_id name  age
1 1       John  19
2 2       Sarah 20
3 3       Jack  21
>
> merged1= merge(issued,user,by='user_id',all.x=T)
> merged1
  user_id issue_id book_id name  age
1 2       1        1       Sarah 20
2 2       2        3       Sarah 20
3 3       3        4       Jack  21
```

The all.x helps to create the create the left join here.
For other joins between two data frames d1 and d2.

```
Inner join     merge(df1, df2, by="common_key_column")
Outer join     merge(df1, df2, by="common_key_column", all=TRUE)
Left outer     merge(df1, df2, by="common_key_column", all.x=TRUE)
Right outer    merge(df1, df2, by="common_key_column", all.y=TRUE)
```

7.4   Summary

SQL can be used in both R and SAS. We can use the sqldf package to use SQL in R and PROC SQL to use SQL in SAS.

The basic syntax for using sql in R is:

```
sqldf('select * from mydata;')
```

The basic syntax for using sql in SAS is:-

```
proc sql number;
select * from mydata;
```

SAS needs data to be sorted before merge. We can also merge data using joins.

7.5   Quiz Questions

1   What does SQL stand for?

2   Name a package that can be used to use SQL in R.

3   Which proc statement is used to use SQL in SAS?

4   Which function is used to combine multiple SQL queries in a single call to sqldf()?

5   What is * used for in the following select statement?

```
select * from mydata;
```

6   Which clause is used to add new values and make changes to a row of a table?

7   Name some SQL constraints.

8 What is HAVING used for in SQL?

9 Name some SQL aggregate functions.

10 Explain the difference between INNER JOIN and LEFT JOIN in SQL.

Quiz Answers

1 Structured Query Language

2 sqldf

3 PROC SQL

4 c()

5 * is used to select all columns from a data table.

6 Sql UPDATE is used to make changes to the rows of a table and is used with the SET and WHERE clause.

7 NOT NULL, Unique, Primary Key.

8 HAVING is used after GROUP BY to select only certain groups from the grouped aggregate values.

9 min(),max(),avg.(),sum(),count() are some SQL aggregate functions.

10 INNER JOIN is used to select only those records which have matching values in the specified column whereas LEFT JOIN selects all records from the first table along with the records which have matching values in the specified column.

8

Functions, Loops, Arrays, Macros

In this chapter, we study ways to make things more automated by using functions in R and Macro Language in SAS. In addition, we study loops (for and do) as well as arrays in SAS.

8.1 Functions

In R Functions in R are quite easy in Syntax. They are of the form:
FUNCTIONNAME+function(x,y,..parameters){ function description}
They are called by FUNCTIONNAME(input value)

```
> a1=function(x){x^3+3^x+5}

> a1(10)
[1] 60054

> a2=function(x,y){x^3+3^y+5}

> a2(10,5)
[1] 1248
```

In SAS we use Proc FMCP.

The FCMP procedures are used to write, compile, and test DATA step functions and CALL routines that can be used in DATA step. For more information, you can read http://support.sas.com/resources/papers/proceedings13/139-2013.pdf

8.2 Loops

Loops are used for tasks that are repeatable. You can also use functions within iterations of loops. Note in SAS you need to use **end** to close loop and **output** to output data.

SAS for R Users: A Book for Data Scientists, First Edition. Ajay Ohri.
© 2020 John Wiley & Sons, Inc. Published 2020 by John Wiley & Sons, Inc.

In SAS:

```
data ajay;
do i =1 to 10;
        Output;
end;
        run;

proc print data=ajay;
run;

Obs     i
1       1
2       2
3       3
4       4
5       5
6       6
7       7
8       8
9       9
10      10

data ajay2 (drop=i);
do i=1 to 10;
 y=i**3+3**i+5;
        output;
        end;
        run;

proc print data=ajay2;
run;

Obs     y
1       9
2       22
3       59
4       150
5       373
6       950
7       2535
8       7078
9       20417
10      60054
```

In R:

```
> for (i in 1:10){print(i)}
[1] 1
[1] 2
[1] 3
[1] 4
[1] 5
[1] 6
[1] 7
[1] 8
[1] 9
[1] 10

> a1=function(x){x^3+3^x+5}

> for (i in 1:10){print(a1(i))}

[1] 9
[1] 22
[1] 59
[1] 150
[1] 373
[1] 950
[1] 2535
[1] 7078
[1] 20417
[1] 60054
```

8.3 Arrays

A **SAS array** is a way of creating a temporary group of variables for processing within a data step for repeatable operations. Arrays help simplify SAS code readability.

Example:
```
array balance[12] bal1-bal12;
```
Here array named balance has 12 variables from variable bal. 1 to bal. 12.

Or
```
ARRAY months {12} $ 12 mth1-mth12 ('January' 'February' 'March'
'April' 'May' 'June' 'July' 'August' 'September' 'October'
'November' 'December');.
```

You can also use * within the number of variables [].

Here we use sashelp dataset pricedata and convert prices from USD to INR

```
data price ;
set sashelp.pricedata;

array price_inr{17} price_inr1-price_inr17;
array price_usd{17} price1-price17;

do i = 1 to 17;
price_inr{i} = price_usd{i}*70;
end;
run;

proc print data= price (obs=5);
var price_inr1-price_inr3 price1-price3;
run;
```

Obs	price_inr1	price_inr2	price_inr3	price1	price2	price3
1	3661.00	8050	2338.0	52.300	115	33.40
2	3661.00	8050	2338.0	52.300	115	33.40
3	3661.00	8050	2338.0	52.300	115	33.40
4	3661.00	8050	1987.3	52.300	115	28.39
5	3111.85	8050	2338.0	44.455	115	33.40

8.4 Macros

The Macro Language is a useful and unique tool within SAS language which helps to reduce SAS code, improve readability and pass data in an automated manner. It is composed of Macro variables and Macro Programs.

Let us take a basic Macro.

Symbolgen option Specifies whether the results of resolving macro variable references are written to the SAS log. That is useful for debugging especially if SAS Macro code shows an error at some part.
```
options symbolgen ;
```

Here we create a macro (named ajay) with one defined variable (i)

Note within the Macro i is referred by &i which denotes it is a macro variable

We use %mend to close the Macro

We then call the Macro using %macroname (here %ajay)

```
%macro ajay(i);

data new1;
do j= 1 to &i;
output;
end;
run;

proc print data=new1;
run;
%mend;

%ajay(5);
```

Let's makes a global macro variable (outside the declared macro)

```
%let name='ajay';
options symbolgen ;
%macro ajay(i);

data new1;
newname=&name;
age=&i*&i;
run;

proc print data=new1;
run;
%mend;

%ajay(5);

Obs      newname      age
1        ajay         25
```

Or, we can dynamically assign dataset paths

```
%let pathfile = '/home/ajay4/book';
libname macro1 &pathfile;
run;
```

The SAS log shows the following

```
71     %let pathfile = '/home/ajay4/book';
72     libname macro1 &pathfile;
SYMBOLGEN: Macro variable PATHFILE resolves to
'/home/ajay4/book'

NOTE: Libref MACRO1 was successfully assigned as follows:
   Engine: V9
   Physical Name: /home/ajay4/book
73     run;
```

We can use multiple words for %let. We can also &SYSDATE and &SYSDAY for todays date and day respectively

```
%let use = EngineSize Invoice MPG_City ;

title "Today's date is &SYSDATE9 and day is &SYSDAY";

proc means data=sashelp.cars mean;
var &use;
run;
```

Today's date is 12DEC2018 and day is Wednesday

The MEANS Procedure

Variable	Label	Mean
EngineSize	Engine Size (L)	3.1967290
Invoice		30 014.70
MPG_City	MPG (City)	20.0607477

%PUT: This statement writes the text in SAS log.

```
%put &name;
%put &use;
```

From SAS Log

```
SYMBOLGEN: Macro variable NAME resolves to 'ajay'
70
71 %put &name;
'ajay'
72 %put &use;
SYMBOLGEN: Macro variable USE resolves to EngineSize
  Invoice MPG_City
EngineSize Invoice MPG_City
```

We can also do string operations using Macro variables.

1) **%upcase**: converts into upper case.
2) **%substr**: returns characters from specified position.
3) **%scan**: returns the variable whose number is specified.

```
options nosymbolgen;
%put &use;
%let newuse =%UPCASE(&use);
%put &newuse;

%let new2=%scan(&newuse,3);
%put &new2 ;

%let subword=%substr(&newuse, 3,5);
%put &subword;

71     options nosymbolgen;
72     %put &use;
EngineSize Invoice MPG_City

73     %let newuse =%UPCASE(&use);
74     %put &newuse;
ENGINESIZE INVOICE MPG_CITY

75
76     %let new2=%scan(&newuse,3);
77     %put &new2 ;
MPG_CITY

78
79     %let subword=%substr(&newuse, 3,5);
80     %put &subword;
GINES
```

Data _null_: To gain higher efficiency in a SAS program, creation of additional dataset can be avoided using this statement. It creates a null dataset.

CALL SYMPUT: This function assigns data step information to a macro variable. It has two parts:

1) This specifies a character expression that identifies the macro variable which is assigned a value. If the macro variable does not exist, the routine creates it.
2) This specifies a character constant, variable, or expression that contains the value that is assigned.

Here ODS helps create an output in an excel file while other macro variables help create the path for a file. Instead of proc. sort we can also put more elaborate analytical statements here.

```
%let pathfile = '/home/ajay4/book' ;
libname auto &pathfile;
run;
options compress=yes;
options symbolgen;
%macro impmth(mth,num);
data _null_ ;
/* call symput('unqxls',"'"||&pathfile||"unq"
||&mth||'.xls'||"'" ); */
call symput('unqxls',"'"||'.xls'||"'" );
run;

proc sort data=auto.&num nodupkey;
by user_id;
run;

ODS HTML FILE=&unqxls;
proc print data=auto.&num;
run;
ODS HTML CLOSE;
%mend;

%impmth(01,issued)
```

8.5   Quiz Questions

1   How do we close a do loop in SAS?

2   How we get output in a do loop in SAS?

3   How do we create a function with two parameters in R?

4   How do we close a macro in SAS?

5   What command in data step helps create a null dataset?

6   How do I output macro variables in SAS log?

7   With which option do we print out macro variables in an SAS log?

8   Which function gives data step information to a macro variable?

9　Which function can be used to create output in excel format in SAS?

10　Which function can be used to create a global macro variable?

Quiz Answers

1　End

2　Output

3　function(x,y){commands}

4　%mend

5　Data _null_

6　%put

7　Symbolgen

8　Call symput

9　ODS HTML

10　%let

9

Data Visualization

Data Visualization is an important part of the data science process. Here we learn how to do data science in both languages.

9.1 Importance of Data Visualization

The anscombe dataset shows the importance of data visualization. On statistical examination it shows data is similar. But on visualization it shows the data is very different.

Property	Value
Mean of x	9
Sample variance of x	11
Mean of y	7.50
Sample variance of y	4.125
Correlation between x and y	0.816
Linear regression line	$y = 3.00 + 0.500x$
Coefficient of determination of the linear regression	0.67

But the graphs are quite different.

```
data("anscombe")
attach(anscombe) #attaching dataset so we dont have to use $
par(mfrow=c(2,2)) #setting number of plots in page
par(bg='gray')
plot(x1,y1,col='red')
plot(x2,y2,col='red')
plot(x3,y3,col='red')
plot(x4,y4,col='red')
```

SAS for R Users: A Book for Data Scientists, First Edition. Ajay Ohri.
© 2020 John Wiley & Sons, Inc. Published 2020 by John Wiley & Sons, Inc.

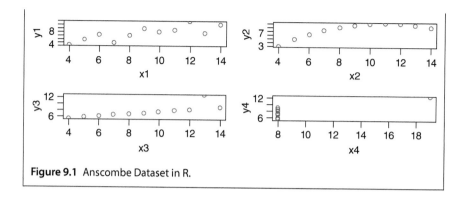

Figure 9.1 Anscombe Dataset in R.

We are going to do the following graphs in this chapter for both SAS and R:

- Bar Plot: A **bar** chart represents data in vertical **bars** with height of the **bar** proportional to the value of the variable.
- Bar-Line Plot: A combination of Bar Plots with Line Graphs, with one quantity being represented in a Bar Plot and the other in a Line Graph.
- Box Plot: A plot in which a rectangle is drawn to represent the second and third quartiles, usually with a vertical line inside to indicate the median value.
- Bubble Plot: A bubble chart is a type of chart that displays three dimensions of data. Each entity with its triplet (v_1, v_2, v_3) of associated data is plotted as a disk that expresses two of the v_i values through the disk's xy location and the third through its size.
- Heat Map: A plot in which data values are represented as colors.
- Histogram: This represents the frequencies of a variable bucketed into breaks.
- Line Chart: A graph that connects a series of points by drawing lines between them.
- Mosaic Plot: A graphical display of the cell frequencies of a contingency table in which the area of boxes of the plot are proportional to the cell frequencies.
- Pie Chart: A pie chart (or a circle chart) is a circular statistical graphic, which is divided into slices to illustrate numerical proportion.
- Scatter Plot: A graph in which the values of two variables are plotted along two axes, the pattern of the resulting points revealing any correlation present.

9.2   Data Visualization in SAS

The Tasks and Utilities option in SAS Studio enables graphs quite easily as well as generation of code. Due to printability options we are giving partial output here.

SAS® Studio

▸ Server Files and Folders

▾ Tasks and Utilities

▸ My Tasks

◢ Tasks

　▸ Data

　◢ Graph

　　Bar Chart

　　Bar-Line Chart

　　Box Plot

　　Bubble Plot

　　Heat Map

　　Histogram

　　Line Chart

　　Mosaic Plot

　　Pie Chart

　　Scatter Plot

　　Series Plot

Figure 9.2 Data Visualization Options in SAS.

Bar Plot:

```
ods graphics / reset width=6.4in height=4.8in imagemap;

proc sgplot data=SASHELP.IRIS;
     vbar Species / group=SepalLength groupdisplay=cluster;
     yaxis grid;
run;

ods graphics / reset;
```

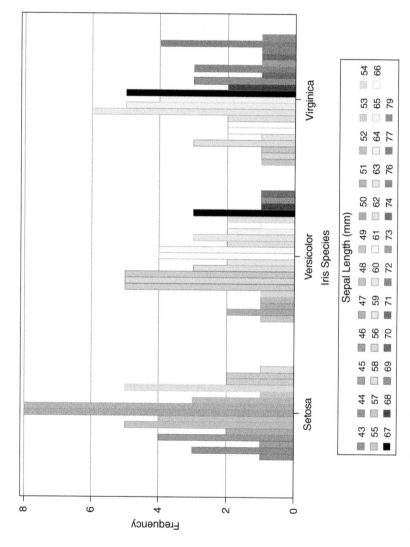

Figure 9.3 Bar Plot in SAS.

Bar- Line Plot:

```
/* Compute axis ranges */
proc means data=SASHELP.IRIS noprint;
     class Species / order=data;
     var SepalLength PetalLength;
     output out=_BarLine_(where=(_type_ > 0)) mean(SepalLength
       PetalLength)=resp1
             resp2;
run;

/* Compute response min and max values (include 0 in
computations) */
data _null_;
     retain respmin 0 respmax 0;
     retain respmin1 0 respmax1 0 respmin2 0 respmax2 0;
     set _BarLine_ end=last;
     respmin1=min(respmin1, resp1);
     respmin2=min(respmin2, resp2);
     respmax1=max(respmax1, resp1);
     respmax2=max(respmax2, resp2);

     if last then
               do;
                   call symputx ("respmin1", respmin1);
                   call symputx ("respmax1", respmax1);
                   call symputx ("respmin2", respmin2);
                   call symputx ("respmax2", respmax2);
                   call symputx ("respmin", min(respmin1,
                     respmin2));
                   call symputx ("respmax", max(respmax1,
                     respmax2));
               end;
run;

/* Define a macro for offset */
%macro offset ();
     %if %sysevalf(&respmin eq 0) %then
               %do;
                   offsetmin=0 %end;
     %if %sysevalf(&respmax eq 0) %then
               %do;
                   offsetmax=0 %end;
%mend offset;
```

```
ods graphics / reset width=6.4in height=4.8in imagemap;
proc sgplot data=SASHELP.IRIS nocycleattrs;
    vbar Species / response=SepalLength
      fillattrs=(color=CX6c0a00) stat=mean;
    vline Species / response=PetalLength lineattrs=(thickness=5)
      stat=mean y2axis;
    yaxis grid min=&respmin1 max=&respmax1 %offset();
    y2axis min=&respmin2 max=&respmax2 %offset();
    keylegend / location=outside;
run;
```

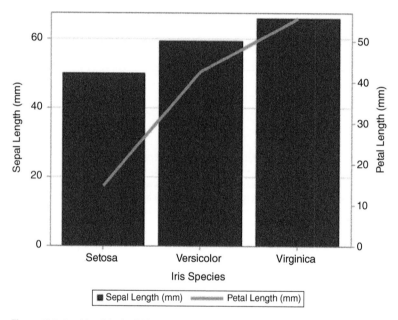

Figure 9.4 Bar-Line Plot in SAS.

Box Plot:

```
ods graphics / reset width=6.4in height=4.8in imagemap;

proc sgplot data=SASHELP.IRIS;
        vbox SepalLength / category=Species fillattrs=
        (color=CX68000f);
        yaxis grid;
run;

ods graphics / reset;
```

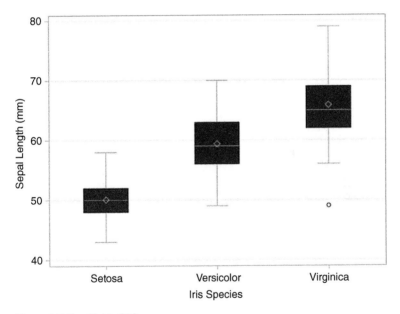

Figure 9.5 Box Plot in SAS.

Bubble Plot:

```
ods graphics / reset width=6.4in height=4.8in imagemap;

proc sgplot data=SASHELP.IRIS;
      bubble x=SepalLength y=SepalWidth size=PetalLength/
         group=Species bradiusmin=7
            bradiusmax=14;
      xaxis grid;
      yaxis grid;
run;

ods graphics / reset;
```

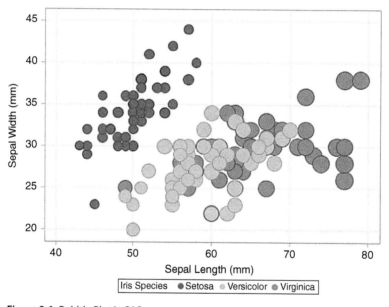

Figure 9.6 Bubble Plot in SAS.

Heat Map:

```
ods graphics / reset width=6.4in height=4.8in imagemap;

proc sgplot data=SASHELP.IRIS;
        heatmap x=SepalLength y=PetalLength / name='HeatMap'
          colorresponse=PetalWidth;
        gradlegend 'HeatMap';
run;

ods graphics / reset;
```

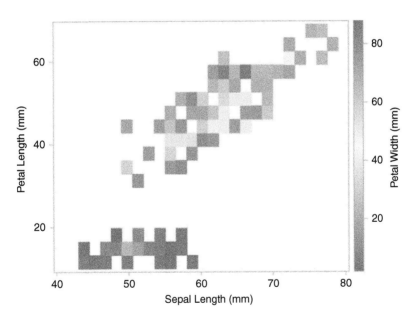

Figure 9.7 Heat Map in SAS.

Histogram:

```
ods graphics / reset width=6.4in height=4.8in imagemap;

proc sgplot data=SASHELP.IRIS;
        histogram SepalLength /;
        density SepalLength;
        yaxis grid;
run;

ods graphics / reset;
```

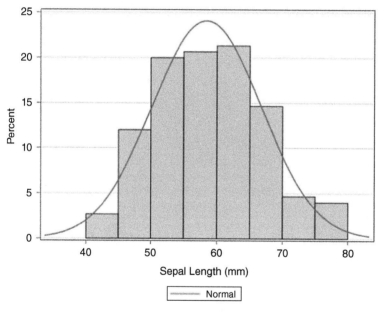

Figure 9.8 Histogram in SAS.

Line Chart:

```
ods graphics / reset width=6.4in height=4.8in imagemap;

proc sgplot data=SASHELP.IRIS;
        vline SepalLength / curvelabel lineattrs=(thickness=4
          color=CX99002e)
                transparency=0.5;
        yaxis grid;
run;

ods graphics / reset;
```

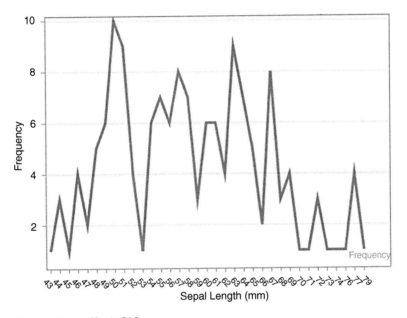

Figure 9.9 Line Plot in SAS.

Mosaic Plot:

```
ods noproctitle;

proc freq data=SASHELP.CARS;
      ods select MosaicPlot;
      tables Cylinders*Type / plots=mosaicplot;
run;
```

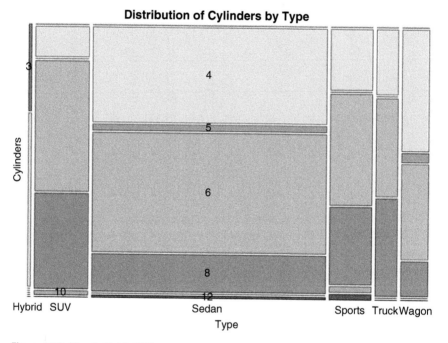

Figure 9.10 Mosaic Plot in SAS.

Pie Chart:

```
proc template;
     define statgraph SASStudio.Pie;
          begingraph;
          layout region;
          piechart category=Cylinders /;
          endlayout;
          endgraph;
        end;
run;

ods graphics / reset width=6.4in height=4.8in imagemap;

proc sgrender template=SASStudio.Pie data=SASHELP.CARS;
run;

ods graphics / reset;
```

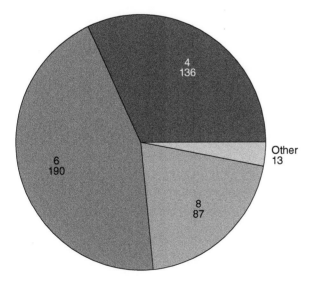

Figure 9.11 Pie Plot in SAS.

Scatter Plot:

```
ods graphics / reset width=6.4in height=4.8in imagemap;

proc sgplot data=SASHELP.CARS;
        scatter x=MPG_City y=Type /;
        xaxis grid;
        yaxis grid;
run;

ods graphics / reset;
```

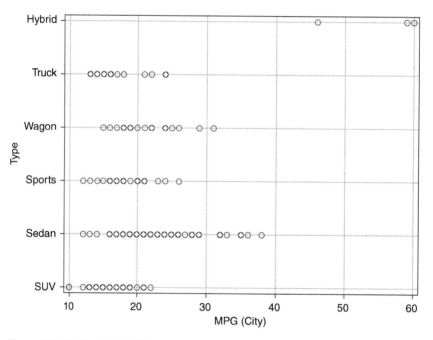

Figure 9.12 Scatter Plot in SAS.

9.3   Data Visualization in R

Bar Plot:

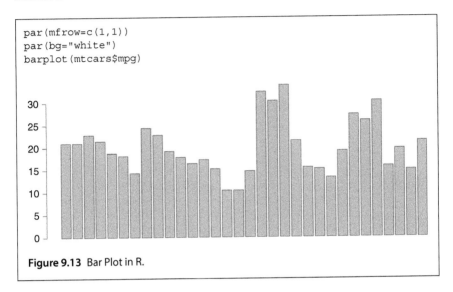

```
par(mfrow=c(1,1))
par(bg="white")
barplot(mtcars$mpg)
```

Figure 9.13 Bar Plot in R.

Bar-Line Plot:

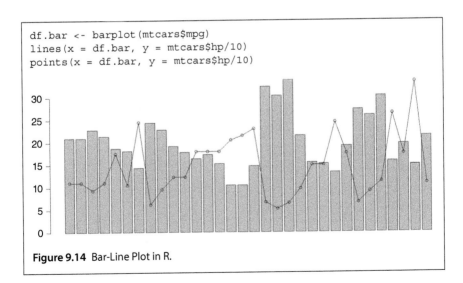

```
df.bar <- barplot(mtcars$mpg)
lines(x = df.bar, y = mtcars$hp/10)
points(x = df.bar, y = mtcars$hp/10)
```

Figure 9.14 Bar-Line Plot in R.

Box Plot:

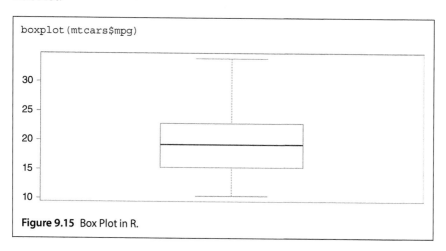

Figure 9.15 Box Plot in R.

Bubble Plot:

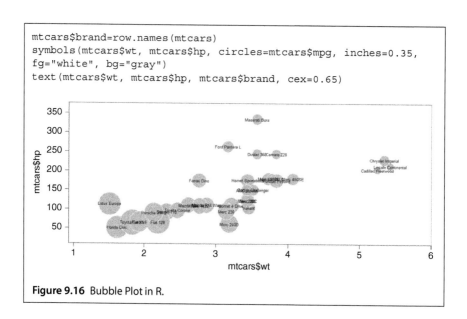

Figure 9.16 Bubble Plot in R.

Heat Map:

```
data(mtcars)
mtscaled <- as.matrix(scale(mtcars))
# create heatmap and don't reorder columns
heatmap(mtscaled, Colv=F, scale='none')
```

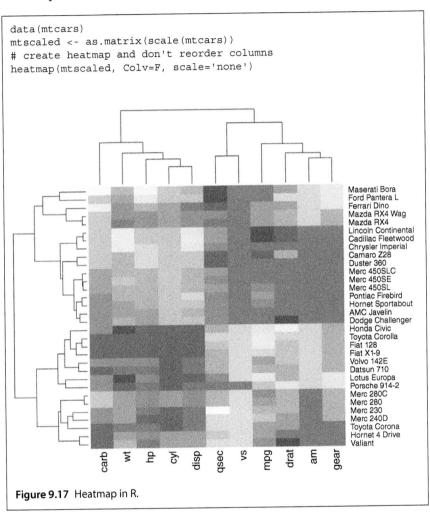

Figure 9.17 Heatmap in R.

Histogram:

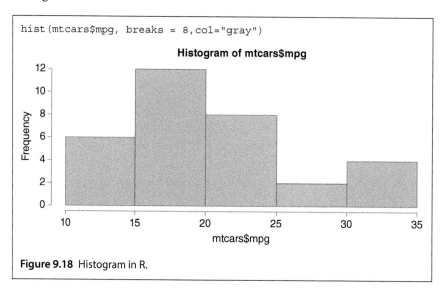

Figure 9.18 Histogram in R.

Line Chart:

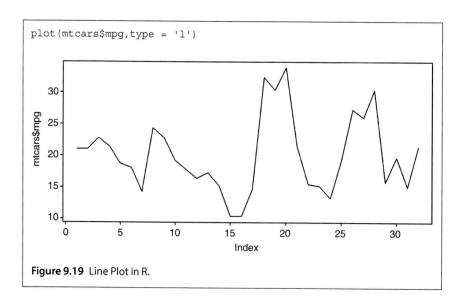

Figure 9.19 Line Plot in R.

Mosaic Plot:

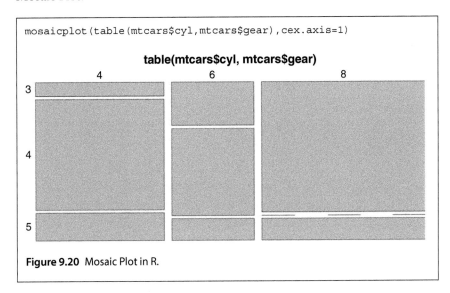

Figure 9.20 Mosaic Plot in R.

Pie Chart:

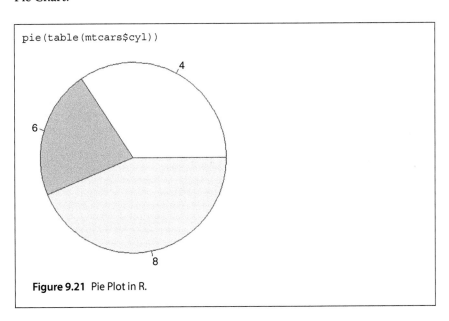

Figure 9.21 Pie Plot in R.

Scatter Plot:

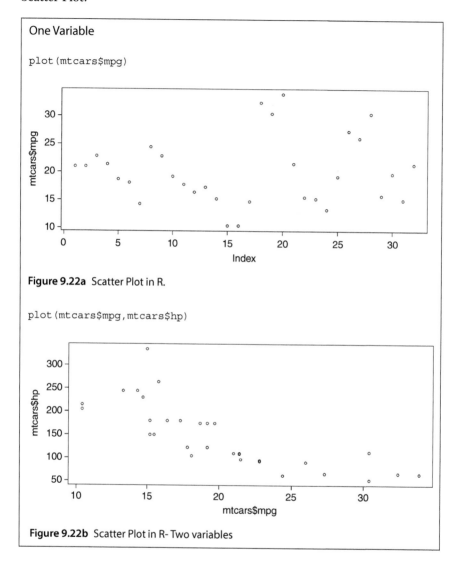

One Variable

```
plot(mtcars$mpg)
```

Figure 9.22a Scatter Plot in R.

```
plot(mtcars$mpg,mtcars$hp)
```

Figure 9.22b Scatter Plot in R- Two variables

9.4 Quiz Questions

1 What type of plot shows inter quartile range and median?

2 What type of plot shows relative numerical quantities in terms of height?

3 Which type of plot connects points with lines?

4 Which type of plot shows relative frequency of two or more categorical variables through area?

5 Which type of graph shows frequencies as grouped in breaks?

6 Which type of graph shows color intensity as a measure of variable quantity?

7 Which type of graph can show three and even four quantities?

8 Which type of graph shows relative frequencies as a circle?

9 Where do Graphs appear in SAS Studio?

10 What does Anscombe dataset prove?

Quiz Answers

1 Boxplot

2 Barplot

3 Line Plot

4 Mosaic Plot

5 Histogram

6 HeatMap

7 Bubble Plot

8 Pie Chart

9 Tasks and Utilities in the left pane

10 Pure numerical statistics can be deceptive without data visualization.

10

Data Output

Output is very important in analysis to show the results of data science to stakeholders. It can primarily be Excel, Powerpoint, and Word documents for data analysis. With the advent of cloud and collaboration tools, there are many ways to communicate the intermediate stages of data analysis. The following shows ways to show output in R and SAS.

10.1 Data Output in SAS

There are two ways:

1) Proc Export- Proc Export can export data in many formats

```
PROC EXPORT DATA= datasetname
        OUTFILE= "location and file name.XLS"
        DBMS=EXCEL REPLACE;
   SHEET="excel worksheet name";
RUN;
```

Here, replace will replace an earlier file with same name

2) ODS
   ODS stands for output delivery system. It is used to format the output of a SAS program. We can output data by putting output print within ODS HTML and ODS HTML CLOSE. Here we output the PROC Means of a dataset to a different object and print it to an excel file.

```
ODS HTML FILE= '/home/ajay4/sasuser.v94/cars.xls';
Proc means data=mtcars; output out=carsmeans; run;
proc. print data=carsmean; run;
ODS HTML CLOSE;
```

SAS for R Users: A Book for Data Scientists, First Edition. Ajay Ohri.
© 2020 John Wiley & Sons, Inc. Published 2020 by John Wiley & Sons, Inc.

3) Images

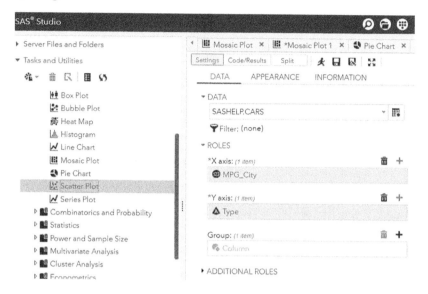

Figure 10.1 Creating plots in SAS.

Output is in the form of an HTML page which can be saved.

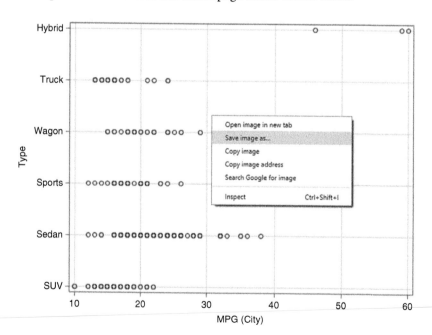

Figure 10.2 HTML output plot in SAS.

10.2 Data Output in R

Here we change a working directory to the output folder. We take an object (or create an output dataframe, or object, then output them write.csv (just as we used read.cev to input data).

```
> getwd()
[1] "C:/Users/ajaohri/Documents"

> setwd("C:/Users/ajaohri/Desktop")

> data(iris)
> write.csv(iris,"iris.csv")

> dir(pattern='csv')
[1] "airquality.csv" "iris.csv" "mtcars.csv"
```

We can also use fwrite in the data table package.

```
> library(data.table)

> fwrite(iris,"iris2.csv")

> dir(pattern='csv')
    [1] "airquality.csv" "iris.csv" "iris2.csv" "mtcars.csv"
```

We can also use write_csv in readr package

```
> library(readr)

> write_csv(iris,"iris3.csv")

> dir(pattern='csv')
[1] "airquality.csv" "iris.csv" "iris2.csv" "iris3.csv"
    [5] "mtcars.csv"
```

For Graphs we can export plots in 3 Ways in RStudio: Picture, PDF, and Copy to Clipboard.

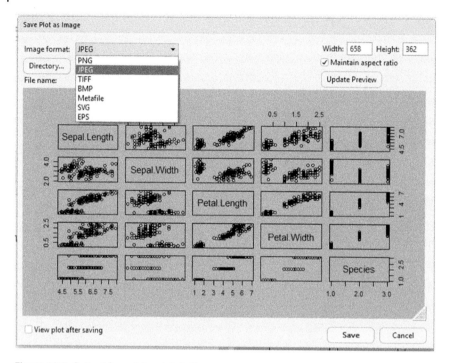

Figure 10.3 Output format for plots in R.

However, there are seven types of images.

We can also have html, pdf and word output of code and output. We can download them locally and also publish it on RPubs; a repository website provided by RStudio.

html output using the knit package/button in RStudio,can be opened in the browser, published and shared on Rpubs.

We have this code:

```
setwd("C:/Users/ajayohri/Desktop")
getwd()
setwd("C:/Users/ajayohri/Documents")
data(iris)
write.csv(iris,"iris.csv")
dir(pattern='csv')
library(data.table)
fwrite(iris,"iris2.csv")
dir(pattern='csv')
```

```
library(readr)
write_csv(iris,"iris3.csv")
dir(pattern='csv')
```

We use knit as follows:

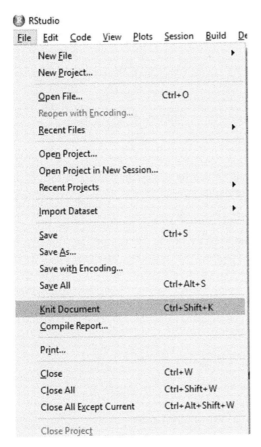

Figure 10.4 Knit document in R studio.

We have three types of output- HTML, Word, PDF by using Knit. Let's take the HTML output here:

This is our output.

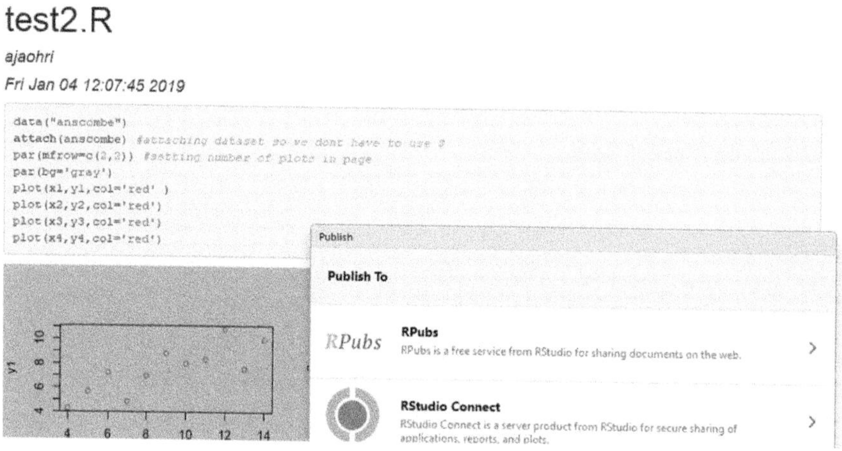

test2.R

ajaohri

Fri Jan 04 12:07:45 2019

```
data("anscombe")
attach(anscombe) #attaching dataset so we dont have to use $
par(mfrow=c(2,2)) #setting number of plots in page
par(bg='gray')
plot(x1,y1,col='red' )
plot(x2,y2,col='red')
plot(x3,y3,col='red')
plot(x4,y4,col='red')
```

Publish

Publish To

RPubs **RPubs**
RPubs is a free service from RStudio for sharing documents on the web.   >

RStudio Connect
RStudio Connect is a server product from RStudio for secure sharing of applications, reports, and plots.   >

Figure 10.5 HTML output by knit in R.

We can open it in the browser on the top left. We can publish it to RPubs using the Publish button on the top right. For secure publishing we can use RConnect.

We can also create Markdown documents of R Code by rmarkdown library.

R Markdown is a file format for making **dynamic documents** with R. An R Markdown document is written in markdown (an easy-to-write **plain text format**) and contains chunks of embedded R code, like the document below. --- output: html_document --- This is an R Markdown document. (see https://rmarkdown.rstudio.com/articles_intro.html)

10.3   Quiz Questions

1   How many types of image formats can be down in RStudio?

2   What package in R can create markdown of R Code?

3   In which website can you publish R Code but privately?

4   What are the three types of output by using knit in RStudio?

5   What command writes data in data. table package in R?

6   What proc. writes data in SAS?

7 What does ODS stand for?

8 How do we close ODS code?

9 How can we save pictures in SAS?

10 What does REPLACE do in Proc Export?

Quiz Answers

1 7

2 rmarkdown

3 R Connect

4 HTML, Word, PDF

5 fwrite

6 Proc Export

7 Output Delivery System

8 ODS HTML Close

9 Saving Image from a HTML page

10 Replaces the file with existing name in PROC EXPORT so program can be run repeatedly.

11

Statistics for Data Scientists

Data Scientists need to study statistics as well as computer science to be effective in their analytical journey.

11.1   Types of Variables

1) **QUANTITATIVE VARIABLES**: Data that consists of counts or measurements. You can perform arithmetic operations on them. There are two types:
   a) Discrete Variable has a countable number of values within a specified range. For example, 14, 15, 17.
   b) Continuous Variable has an infinite number of values without any break or jump. For example, 14–16 (this includes 14.001 and also 14.0000001).

2) **CATEGORICAL VARIABLES**: Variables that denote groupings or labels. Arithmetic operations cannot be performed on them.
   a) Nominal Variable has no ordering within its observed levels, groups, or categories. For example, gender (male and female cannot be ordered).
   b) Ordinal Variable has meaningful ordering within its levels. For example, Disease condition divided into categories of low, moderate, or severe.

SAS for R Users: A Book for Data Scientists, First Edition. Ajay Ohri.
© 2020 John Wiley & Sons, Inc. Published 2020 by John Wiley & Sons, Inc.

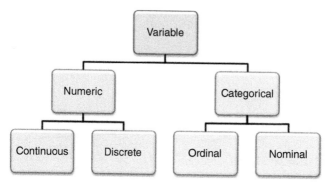

Figure 11.1 Variable types.

11.2 Statistical Methods for Data Analysis

Two main statistical methods are used in data analysis: descriptive statistics, which summarize data from a sample using indexes such as the mean or standard deviation, and inferential statistics, which draw conclusions from data that are subject to random variation (e.g. observational errors, sampling variation)

Descriptive statistics	Inferential statistics
organize, describe, and summarize data using numbers and graphical techniques	concerned with drawing conclusions about a population from analysis of a random sample drawn from that population and also the precision and reliability of those inferences.
Also known as exploratory data analysis	Also known as explanatory modeling
Includes frequency, measures of location, central tendency and measures of dispersion or variability	Includes parameter estimation (through method of moments, method of maximum likelihood etc.) and hypothesis testing (t-test, f-test etc)

11.3 Distributions

Frequency – The frequency of a particular data value is the number of times the data value occurs. For example, if four people have an age of 35, then the age of 35 is said to have a frequency of 4.

A frequency distribution is an overview of all distinct values in some variable and the number of times they occur. That is, a frequency distribution tells how frequencies are distributed over values. Some distributions are below:

1) Normal Distribution – Normal distribution in a variate X with mean mu and variance sigma^2 is a statistic distribution with probability density function. While statisticians and mathematicians uniformly use the term "normal distribution" for this distribution, physicists sometimes call it a Gaussian distribution and, because of its curved flaring shape, social scientists refer to it as the "bell curve."

2) Chi Square – The chi-squared distribution with k degrees of freedom is the distribution of a sum of the squares of k independent standard normal random variables.

3) Bernoulli- It is the probability distribution of a random variable which takes the value 1 with probability {\displaystyle p} p and the value 0 with probability {\displaystyle q=1-p,} {\displaystyle q=1-p,} that is, the probability distribution of any single experiment that asks a yes–no question.

4) Poisson – The Poisson distribution is the discrete probability distribution of the number of events occurring in a given time period, given the average number of times the event occurs over that time period.

11.4   Descriptive Statistics

Statistics that describe data are descriptive statistics as shown below.

11.4.1   Measures of Central Tendency: It is the Measure of Location that Gives an Overall Idea of the Dataset

1) Mean – The sum of the values divided by the number of values.

2) Median – The median is the value separating the higher half from the lower half of a data sample. For a dataset, it may be thought of as the "middle" value. For example, in the data set {1, 3, 3, 5, 7, 8, 9}, the median is 5.

3) Mode – The number which appears most often in a set of numbers. For example: in {7, 3, 8, 7, 7, 5, 9, 3} the Mode is 7 as its frequency is the most (it occurs most often).

11.4.2   Measures of Dispersion

1) Range – The difference between the lowest and highest values.

2) Quartiles – The values that divide a list of numbers into quarters (four parts).

3) Variance – The average of the squared differences from the Mean.

4) Standard Deviation – The standard deviation is the square root of the variance.

11.4.3 Skewness and Kurtosis

Skewness – Asymmetry in a statistical distribution.

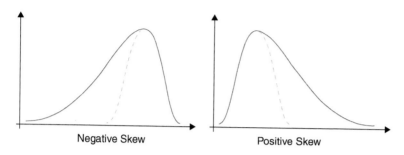

Kurtosis – a measure of the degree of "peaking" in a distribution curve.

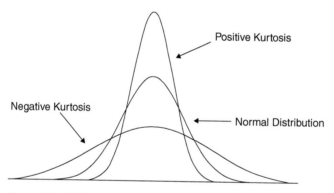

Figure 11.2 (a) Skewness and (b) kurtosis.

11.4.4 Central Limit Theorem

In probability theory, the central limit theorem establishes that, in some situations, when independent random variables are added, their properly normalized sum tends toward a normal distribution even if the original variables themselves are not normally distributed.

11.5 Inferential Statistics

Inferential statistics use a random sample of data taken from a population to describe and make inferences about the population.

11.5.1   Hypothesis Testing

Hypothesis testing is the use of statistics to determine the probability that a given hypothesis is true. The usual process of hypothesis testing consists of four steps.

1) Formulate the null hypothesis H_0 (commonly, that the observations are the result of pure chance) and the alternative hypothesis H_a (commonly, that the observations show a real effect combined with a component of chance variation).
2) Identify a test statistic that can be used to assess the truth of the null hypothesis.
3) Compute the P-value, which is the probability that a test statistic at least as significant as the one observed would be obtained assuming that the null hypothesis were true. The smaller the P-value, the stronger the evidence against the null hypothesis.
4) Compare the *p*-value to an acceptable significance value alpha (sometimes called an alpha value). If $p<=$alpha, that the observed effect is statistically significant, the null hypothesis is ruled out, and the alternative hypothesis is valid.

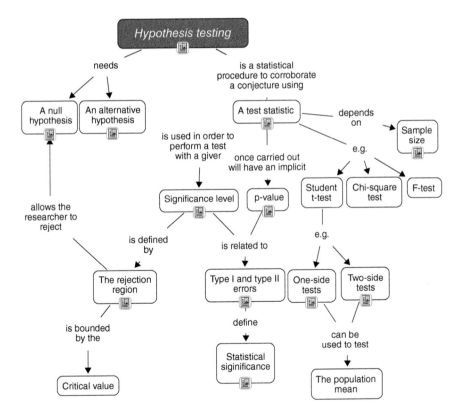

Figure 11.3 Hypotheis test types.

Type 1 and Type 2 Error – There are two types of error statistically. a type I error is the rejection of a true null hypothesis (also known as a "false positive" finding), while a type II error is failing to reject a false null hypothesis (also known as a "false negative" finding).

	Null hypothesis is TRUE	Null hypothesis is FALSE
Reject null hypothesis	Type I Error (False positive)	Correct outcome! (True positive)
Fail to reject null hypothesis	Correct outcome! (True negative)	Type II Error (False negative)

Figure 11.4 Types of statistical error.

Statistical Tests

These tests apply to two samples. The paired two sample tests assume that we have two samples or observations, and that we are testing for a change, usually from one time period to another.

Distribution of the Data

* Kolmogorov-Smirnov Non-parametric Are the distributions different?
* Wilcoxon Signed Rank Non-parametric Do paired samples have different distribution?

Location of the Average

* T-test   Parametric   Are the means different?
* Wilcoxon Rank-Sum Non-parametric Are the medians different?

Variation in the Data

* F-test Parametric Are the variances different?

Correlation

* Correlation Pearsons Are the values from the paired samples correlated?

11.5.2 Probability

1) Probability – Probability is defined as the extent to which an event is likely to occur, measured by the ratio of the favorable cases to the whole number of cases possible.
2) Independence – When two events are said to be **independent** of each other, what this means is that the **probability** that one event occurs in no way affects the **probability** of the other event occurring. An example of two **independent** events is as follows; say you rolled a die and flipped a coin.
3) PDF – In probability theory, a probability density function, or density of a continuous random variable, is a function, whose value at any given sample in the sample space can be interpreted as providing a relative likelihood that the value of the random variable would equal that sample.
4) CDF – The cumulative distribution function of a real-valued random variable X, or just distribution function of X, evaluated at x, is the probability that X will take a value less than or equal to x. Furthermore, and by definition, the area under the curve of a PDF(x) between $-\infty$ and x equals its CDF(x).

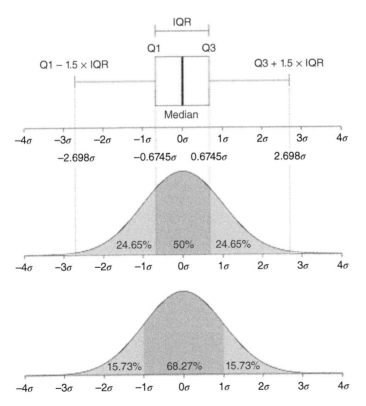

Figure 11.5 Normal distribution.

11.5.3 Bayes Theorem

Bayes' theorem (alternatively Bayes' law or Bayes' rule) describes the probability of an event, based on prior knowledge of conditions that might be related to the event.

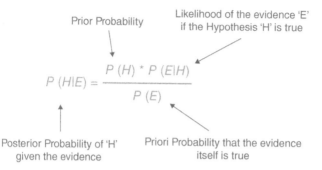

Figure 11.6 Bayes theorem.

11.6 Algorithms in Data Science

Unlike descriptive analytics which describe data of the past predictive analytics deals with forecasts for the future. An algorithm is a set of rules to be followed in calculations of other problem-solving operations, especially by a computer.

SAS has many data mining algorithms in SAS Enterprise Miner. R has a caret package that has many such modeling functions.

What type of problem is it

- If the output of your model is a number, it is a regression problem.
- If the output of your model is a class, it is a classification problem.
- If the output of your model is a set of input groups, it is a clustering problem.
- Linear regression (and other types of regression) is used when the dependent variable is continuous.
- The predictors can be anything (nominal or ordinal categorical, or continuous, or a mix).
- You can also convert independent variables from one type to another.

Factors affecting the choice of a model are

- Whether the model meets the business goals.
- How much pre-processing the model needs.
- How accurate the model is.
- How explainable the model is.

- How fast the model is: How long does it take to build a model, and how long does the model take to make predictions.
- How scalable the model is.

11.6.1 Cross Validation

1) Overfitting – Learning the parameters of a prediction function and testing it on the same data is a methodological mistake: a model that would just repeat the labels of the samples that it has just seen would have a perfect score but would fail to predict anything useful on yet-unseen data. This situation is called overfitting.
2) LeaveOneOut (or LOO) is a simple cross-validation. Each learning set is created by taking all the samples except one, the test set being the sample left out.
3) K-Fold Cross Fitting – Provides train/test indices to split data in train/test sets. Split dataset into k consecutive folds (without shuffling by default). Each fold is then used once as a validation while the k − 1 remaining folds form the training set.

11.6.2 Types of Regression

What is regression? Regression analysis is a set of statistical processes for estimating the relationships among variables.

1) Linear regression – LinearRegression fits a linear model with coefficients to minimize the residual sum of squares between the observed responses in the database. In SAS, we use proc. reg while in R we use lm function.

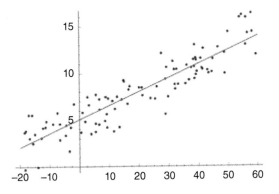

Figure 11.7 Linear regression.

2) Polynomial regression – Uses all polynomial combinations of the features with degree less than or equal to the specified degree. For example, if an input sample is two dimensional and of the form [a, b], the degree-2 polynomial features are [1, a, b, a^2, ab, b^2].

3) Quantile regression – Quantile regression aims at estimating either the conditional median or other quantiles of the response variable.

4) Ridge regression – A regression model where the loss function is the linear least squares function and regularization is given by the l2-norm. Also known as Tikhonov regularization.

5) Lasso regression – Linear Model trained with L1 prior as regularizer (aka the Lasso). The Lasso is a linear model that estimates sparse coefficients. It is useful in some contexts. Lasso method overcomes the disadvantage of Ridge regression by not only punishing high values of the coefficients β but actually setting them to zero if they are not relevant.

6) Elastic Net regression – Linear regression with combined L1 and L2 priors as regularizer. Elastic Net is a linear regression model trained with L1 and L2 prior as regularizer. This combination allows for learning a sparse model where few of the weights are non-zero like Lasso, while still maintaining the regularization properties of Ridge.

7) LAR – Least Angle Regression (LARS) relates to the classic model-selection method known as Forward Selection, or "forward stepwise regression," given a collection of possible predictors, we select the one having largest absolute correlation with the response y. LARS is a regression algorithm for high-dimensional data. LARS is similar to forward stepwise regression. At each step, it finds the predictor most correlated with the response. When there are multiple predictors having equal correlation, instead of continuing along the same predictor, it proceeds in a direction equiangular between the predictors.

11.6.3 Metrics to Evaluate Regression

- The mean_absolute_error function computes mean absolute error, a risk metric corresponding to the expected value of the absolute error loss or - norm loss.

- The mean_squared_error function computes mean square error, a risk metric corresponding to the expected value of the squared (quadratic) error or loss.

- The r2_score function computes R^2, the coefficient of determination. It provides a measure of how well future samples are likely to be predicted by the model. Best possible score is 1.0. A constant model that always predicts the expected value of y, disregarding the input features, would get a R^2 score of 0.0.

11.6.4 Types of Classification

What is classification? Classification is the problem of identifying to which of a set of categories a new observation belongs, on the basis of a training set of data containing observations whose category membership is known.

1) Logistic Regression – In the logistic model, the log-odds (the logarithm of the odds) for the value labeled "1" is a linear combination of one or more independent variables ("predictors"); the independent variables can each be a binary variable (two classes, coded by an indicator variable). In SAS you can do logistic regression using PROC LOGISTIC while R uses glm (see https://stats.idre.ucla.edu/r/dae/logit-regression)

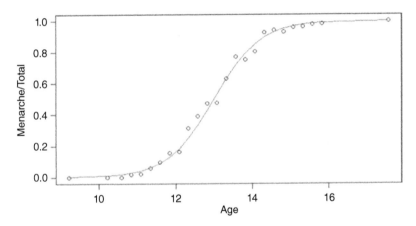

Figure 11.8 Logistic regression.

2) Naive Bayes – These methods are a set of supervised learning algorithms based on applying Bayes' theorem with the "naive" assumption of conditional independence between every pair of features given the value of the class variable.
3) SVM – Support vector machines (SVMs) are a set of supervised learning methods used for classification, regression and outliers detection. An SVM performs classification by finding the hyperplane that maximizes the margin between the two classes. The vectors (cases) that define the hyperplane are the support vector.

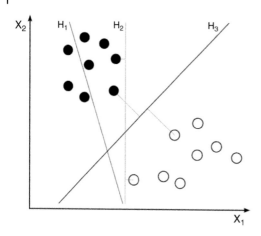

Figure 11.9 Support vector machines SVM.

4) Random Forest – A random forest is a meta estimator that fits a number of decision tree classifiers on various sub-samples of the dataset and uses averaging to improve the predictive accuracy and control over-fitting. The sub-sample size is always the same as the original input sample size but the samples are drawn with replacement if bootstrap=True.

5) kNN – K Nearest Neighbors – The principle behind nearest neighbor methods is to find a predefined number of training samples closest in distance to the new point, and predict the label from these. The number of samples can be a user-defined constant (k-nearest neighbor learning), or vary based on the local density of points (radius-based neighbor learning). The distance can, in general, be any metric measure: standard Euclidean distance is the most common choice.

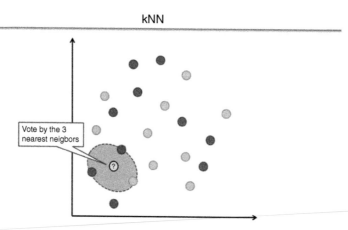

Figure 11.10 k Nearest Neighbors kNN.

6) Decision Trees (DTs) are a non-parametric supervised learning method used for classification and regression. The goal is to create a model that predicts the value of a target variable by learning simple decision rules inferred from the data features.

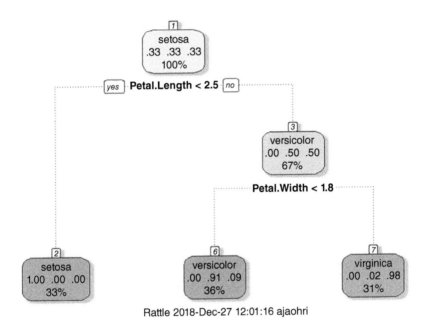

Figure 11.11 Decision tree.

7) XGBoost stands for "Extreme Gradient Boosting." XGBoost is an implementation of gradient boosted DTs designed for speed and performance. A gradient descent procedure is used to minimize the loss when adding trees. Traditionally, gradient descent is used to minimize a set of parameters, such as the coefficients in a regression equation or weights in a neural network. After calculating error or loss, the weights are updated to minimize that error.

11.6.5 Metrics to Evaluate Classification

By definition a confusion matrix C is such that Cij is equal to the number of observations known to be in group i but predicted to be in group j. Thus in binary classification, the count of true negatives is C0,0, false negatives is C1,0, true positives is C1,1 and false positives is C0,1

Confusion Matrix is a 2 X 2 matrix between predicted and actual numbers (for a binary class).

For example:

True positive rate (TPR), Recall, Sensitivity, probability of detection = Σ True positive/Σ Condition positive	False positive rate (FPR), Fall-out, probability of false alarm = Σ False positive/Σ Condition negative
False negative rate (FNR), Miss rate = Σ False negative/Σ Condition positive	Specificity (SPC), Selectivity, True negative rate (TNR) = Σ True negative /Σ Condition negative

		True condition	
	Total population	Condition positive	Condition negative
Predicted condition	Predicted condition positive	**True positive,** Power	**False positive,** Type I error
	Predicted condition negative	**False negative,** Type II error	**True negative**

Figure 11.12 Confusion matrix.

Also see:

- **Precision** = Σ True positive/Σ Predicted condition positive
- **Recall, Sensitivity, probability of detection** = Σ True positive/Σ Condition positive
- **F1 score** = 2/(1/Recall+1/Precision)

Accuracy (ACC) = (Σ True positive + Σ True negative)/Σ Total population

The **precision** is the ratio tp/(tp + fp) where tp is the number of true positives and fp the number of false positives. The precision is intuitively the ability of the classifier not to label as positive a sample that is negative.

The **recall** is the ratio tp/(tp + fn) where tp is the number of true positives and fn the number of false negatives. The recall is intuitively the ability of the classifier to find all the positive samples.

The **F-beta score** can be interpreted as a weighted harmonic mean of the precision and recall, where an F-beta score reaches its best value at 1 and worst score at 0.

The **F-beta score** weights recall more than precision by a factor of beta. Beta == 1.0 means recall and precision are equally important.

The **support** is the number of occurrences of each class in y_true.
A true life confusion matrix is below.

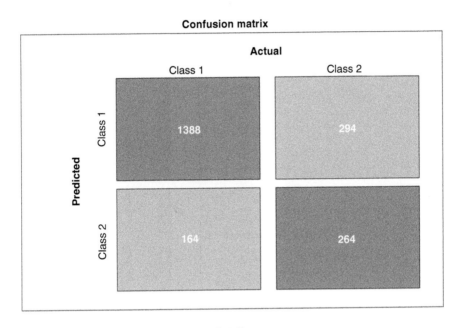

Figure 11.13 Confusion matrix.

A receiver operating characteristic (ROC), or simply ROC curve, is a graphical plot which illustrates the performance of a binary classifier system as its
discrimination threshold is varied. It is created by plotting the fraction of
true positives out of the positives (TPR = true positive rate) vs. the fraction
of false positives out of the negatives (FPR = false positive rate), at various
threshold settings. TPR is also known as sensitivity, and FPR is one minus the
specificity or true negative rate.

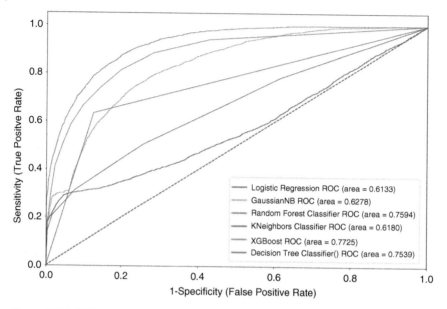

Figure 11.14 ROC curve.

ROC AUC Compute Area Under the Receiver Operating Characteristic Curve (ROC AUC).

11.6.6 Types of Clustering

What is clustering? Clustering is the task of grouping a set of objects in such a way that objects in the same group are more similar to each other than to those in other groups. In SAS, you can use PROC Fastclus while in R you can refer to many functions at the CRAN view of clustering at https://cran.r-project.org/view=Cluster

The following are desirable objectives for any cluster assignment:

1) Homogeneity: each cluster contains only members of a single class.
2) Completeness: all members of a given class are assigned to the same cluster.

There are many types of clustering

1) K Means – The KMeans algorithm clusters data by trying to separate samples in n groups of equal variance, minimizing a criterion known as the inertia or within-cluster sum-of-squares. This algorithm requires the number of clusters to be specified. It scales well to a large number of samples.

K-means clustering on the digits dataset (PCA-reduced data)
Centroids are marked with white cross

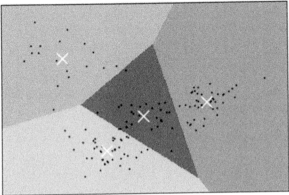

Figure 11.15 K means cluster.

2) Hclust,– Hierarchical clustering is a general family of clustering algorithms that build nested clusters by merging or splitting them successively. This hierarchy of clusters is represented as a tree (or dendrogram). The root of the tree is the unique cluster that gathers all the samples, the leaves being the clusters with only one sample.

The Agglomerative Clustering object performs a hierarchical clustering using a bottom-up approach: each observation starts in its own cluster, and clusters are successively merged together.

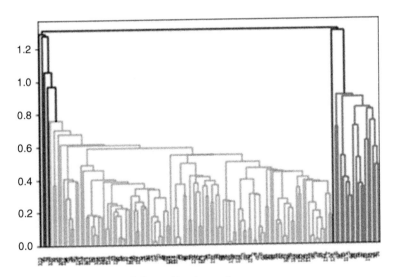

Figure 11.16 Hierachical cluster (dendogram).

3) DBSCAN – The DBSCAN algorithm views clusters as areas of high density separated by areas of low density. Due to this rather generic view, clusters found by DBSCAN can be any shape, as opposed to k-means which assumes that clusters are convex shaped. The central component to the DBSCAN is the concept of core samples, which are samples that are in areas of high density.

4) Gaussian Mixture Models – A Gaussian mixture model is a probabilistic model that assumes all the data points are generated from a mixture of a finite number of Gaussian distributions with unknown parameters. One can think of mixture models as generalizing k-means clustering to incorporate information about the covariance structure of the data as well as the centers of the latent Gaussians.

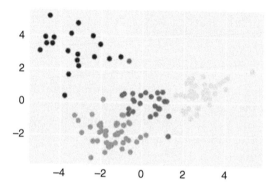

Figure 11.17 Gaussian mixture cluster.

5) Birch – The Birch (Balanced Iterative Reducing and Clustering using Hierarchies) builds a tree called the Characteristic Feature Tree (CFT) for the given data. The data is essentially lossy compressed to a set of Characteristic Feature nodes (CF Nodes). The CF Nodes have a number of subclusters called Characteristic Feature subclusters (CF Subclusters) and these CF Subclusters located in the non-terminal CF Nodes can have CF Nodes as children.

The CF Subclusters hold the necessary information for clustering which prevents the need to hold the entire input data in memory.

6) miniBatch Kmeans – MiniBatchKMeans is a variant of the KMeans algorithm which uses mini-batches to reduce the computation time, while still attempting to optimize the same objective function. Mini-batches are subsets of the input data, randomly sampled in each training iteration. These mini-batches drastically reduce the amount of computation required to converge to a local solution. In contrast to other algorithms that reduce the convergence time of k-means, mini-batch k-means produces results that are generally only slightly worse than the standard algorithm.

7) Mean Shift – MeanShift clustering aims to discover blobs in a smooth density of samples. It is a centroid based algorithm, which works by updating candidates for centroids to be the mean of the points within a given region. These candidates are then filtered in a post-processing stage to eliminate near-duplicates to form the final set of centroids. Mean shift clustering using a flat kernel.

The Number of Clusters-can be given by Elbow or Silhouette method.

11.6.7 Types of Time Series Analysis

What is time series analysis? A time series is a series of data points indexed in time. Two main goals of time series analysis: (a) identifying the nature of the phenomenon represented by the sequence of observations, and (b) forecasting (predicting future values of the time series variable). Major components of nearly every time series are trend, seasonality, and noise. An additional component to a time series can be cylicality. Cyclicality captures data from macro-economic boom bust cycles and their effect on the quantity to be predicted. The time series can be decomposed and the Decomposition Plot can be shown as follows:

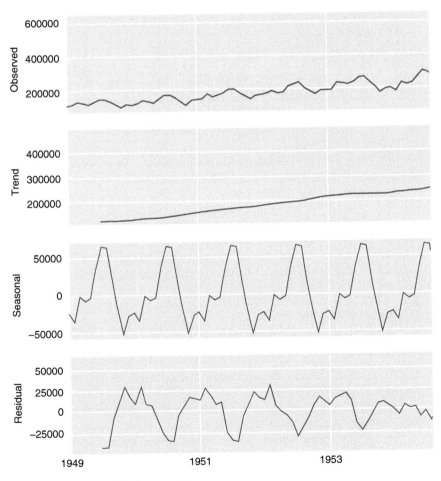

Figure 11.18 Time series decomposition.

Stationarity – A time series is said to be stationary if its **statistical properties** such as mean, and variance remain **constant over time**.

ACF – A plot of ρ_j against j is called the autocorrelation function (**ACF**).

PACF – The **partial autocorrelation function (PACF)** gives the partial correlation of a time series with its own lagged values, controlling for the values of the time series at all shorter lags. It contrasts with the ACF, which does not control for other lags

1) SMA – To estimate the trend component of a non-seasonal time series that can be described using an additive model, it is common to use a smoothing method, such as calculating the simple moving average of the time series.

2) ETS – Exponential Smoothing is a technique to make forecasts by using a weighted mean of past values, wherein more recent values are given higher weights. Whereas in the simple moving average the past observations are weighted equally, exponential functions are used to assign exponentially decreasing weights over time. ETS also stands for error, trend, seasonality models. The first letter is the error type ("A," "M," or "Z"); the second letter is the trend type ("N," "A," "M," or "Z"); and the third letter is the season type ("N," "A," "M," or "Z"). In all cases, "N" = none, "A" = additive, "M" = multiplicative and "Z" = automatically selected.
   a) Simple.
   b) Holt – This extends simple exponential smoothing to allow forecasting of data with a trend.
   c) Winter – The Holt-Winters seasonal method comprises the forecast equation and three smoothing equations – one for the level, one for trend, and one for the seasonal component, with smoothing parameters.

3) ARIMA – ARIMA models or Autoregressive Integration Moving Average models (integration here is the reverse of differencing). Linear exponential smoothing models are all special cases of ARIMA models. The non-linear exponential smoothing models have no equivalent in ARIMA counterparts. ARIMA models are expressed as ARIMA(p,d,q) models, where:

   p = order of the autoregressive part,
   d = degree of first differencing involved,
   q = order of the moving average part.

4) ARIMAX – When an ARIMA model includes other time series such as input variables, the model is sometimes referred to as an ARIMAX model.

5) State Space Models – These models consist. of an equation that describes the observed data and transition equations that describe how the unobserved components or states (level, trend, seasonal) change over time.

6) SSA – Singular spectrum analysis (SSA) which seeks to filter the noise from a given time series, reconstructs a new series which is less noisy, and then uses this newly reconstructed series for forecasting future data points.

7) VAR – Vector autoregressive models. are stochastic process models used to capture the linear interdependencies among multiple time series. VAR models generalize the univariate autoregressive model (AR model) by allowing for more than one evolving variable. All variables in an VAR enter the model in the same way: each variable has an equation explaining its evolution based on its own lagged values, the lagged values of the other model variables, and an error term.

    a) VARIMAX – The VARIMAX Model is a model that the researcher has created to bring three concepts and knowledge, namely, ARIMA Model mixed with VAR Model and the Exogenous Variable used in the model. This is a model that can be used for both good- and short-term forecasting.

8) HMM – Hidden Markov models – The Hidden Markov Model (HMM) is a powerful statistical tool for modeling generative sequences that can be characterized by an underlying process generating an observable sequence. Markov models form a broad and flexible class of models with many possible extensions, while at the same time, allowing for relatively easy analysis and straightforward interpretation. HMM is a statistical Markov model in which the system being modeled is assumed to be a Markov process with unobserved (i.e. hidden) states. The HMM can be represented as the simplest dynamic Bayesian network.

9) Neural Nets – This is a computer system modeled on the human brain and nervous system.

    a) RNN – Recurrent Neural Networks

        i) LSTM – Long Short-Term Memory- (LSTM) units are units of a RNN. An RNN composed of LSTM units is often called an LSTM network. RNN's (LSTM's) are pretty good at extracting patterns in input feature space, where the input data spans over long sequences.

10) Croston – This method involves using simple exponential smoothing (SES) on the non-zero elements of the time series and a separate application of SES to the times between non-zero elements of the time series. It is specialized for dealing with intermittent demand.

11) Composite Method – This involves simple arithmetic combinations of time series.

    Mean absolute percentage error (MAPE), also known as mean absolute percentage deviation (MAPD), is a measure of prediction accuracy of time series.

    In SAS, we can use SAS/ETS for time series forecasting and in R we can use forecast package.

11.6.8 Types of Dimensionality Reduction

What is dimensionality reduction? In very high-dimensional spaces, Euclidean distances tend to become inflated (this is an instance of the so-called "curse of dimensionality").

1) SVD – singular-value decomposition is a factorization of a real or complex matrix. It is the generalization of the Eigendecomposition of a positive semi-definite normal matrix to any matrix via an extension of the polar decomposition.
2) PCA – Principal component analysis (PCA) is a statistical procedure that uses an orthogonal transformation to convert a set of observations of possibly correlated variables (entities each of which takes on various numerical values) into a set of values of linearly uncorrelated variables called principal components.
3) t-SNe – t-Distributed Stochastic Neighbor Embedding (t-SNE) is a tool to visualize high-dimensional data. It converts similarities between data points to joint probabilities and tries to minimize the Kullback–Leibler divergence between the joint probabilities of the low-dimensional embedding and the high-dimensional data. t-SNE has a cost function that is not convex, i.e. with different initializations we can obtain different results.

11.6.9 Types of Text Mining

What is text mining? The process of deriving high-quality information from text.

1) Some concepts
   a) Corpus – a collection of texts.
   b) Term document matrix (TDM) – a mathematical matrix that describes the frequency of terms that occur in a collection of documents.
   c) Word cloud – A visual representation of text data, typically used to depict keyword metadata on websites, or to visualize free-form text. Tags are usually single words, and the importance of each tag is shown with font size or color.
   d) TF-IDF – Tf-idf stands for term frequency-inverse document frequency, and the tf-idf weight is a weight often used in information retrieval and text mining.
   e) Association – It finds the correlation with every other word in a TDM or DTM (Document Term Matrix).
   f) Clustering of Text – Clustering groups similar observations in clusters in order to be able to extract insights from vast amounts of unstructured data.

g) Cosine similarity – Cosine similarity is a measure of similarity between two non-zero vectors of an inner product space that measures the cosine of the angle between them. The cosine of $0°$ is 1.

h) Ngram – a contiguous sequence of n items from a given sample of text or speech.

2) Sentiment Analysis – Identifying and categorizing opinions expressed in text, especially r to determine whether the text is positive, negative, or neutral in sentiment to a particular topic.

3) Web Scraping – A technique employed to extract large amounts of data from the Internet to be saved locally.

4) Topic Modeling – A type of statistical modeling for discovering the "topics" that occur in a collection of documents. Latent Dirichlet Allocation (LDA) is an example of topic model.

11.7   Quiz Questions

1   What does ROC stand for?

2   What does SSA stand for?

3   What does BIRCH stand for?

4   What does ARIMA stand for?

5   What does t-SNE stand for?

6   What does HMM stand for?

7   What does RNN stand for?

8   What does LSTM stand for?

9   What does PCA stand for?

10   What does LDA stand for?

Quiz Answers

1   receiver operating characteristic (ROC), or simply ROC curve

2   singular spectrum analysis (SSA)

3 Birch (Balanced Iterative Reducing and Clustering using Hierarchies)

4 ARIMA models or Autoregressive Integration Moving Average

5 t-Distributed Stochastic Neighbor Embedding (t-SNE)

6 Hidden Markov Model (HMM).

7 Recurrent Neural Nets.

8 Long Short-Term Memory- (LSTM).

9 Principal component analysis (PCA).

10 Latent Dirichlet Allocation (LDA) is an example of topic model.

Further Reading

Allaire JJ, Xie Y, McPherson J, Luraschi J, Ushey K, Atkins A, Wickham H, Cheng J, Chang W. 2018 *rmarkdown: Dynamic Documents for R*. R package version 1.10. https://cran.r-project.org/web/packages/rmarkdown/index.html (accessed April 8, 2019).

Brownlee J. Machine Learning Mastery. https://machinelearningmastery.com/ (accessed April 8, 2019).

Hypothesis Testing CMAP. https://cmap.ihmc.us/ (accessed April 8, 2019).

Ohri A. A White Paper on Automated Time Series Forecasting. *ELK Asia Pacific Journals*. 978-81-933908-0-1

Ohri, A. (2012). *R for Business Analytics*. New York: Springer.

Ohri, A. (2014). *R for Cloud Computing*. New York: Springer.

Ohri, A. (2018). *Python for R Users: A Data Science Approach*. Hoboken: Wiley.

Pedregosa, F., Varoquaux, G., Gramfort, A. et al. (2011). Scikit-learn: Machine Learning in Python. *JMLR* 12 (Oct): 2825–2830.

R Core Team (2018). *R: A language and environment for statistical computing*. Vienna, Austria: R Foundation for Statistical Computing https://www.R-project.org/ (accessed April 8, 2019).

R Data Import/Export. http://cran.r-project.org/doc/manuals/r-rlease/R-data. html (accessed April 8, 2019).

RStudio Team (2015). *RStudio: Integrated Development for R*. Boston, MA: RStudio, Inc http://www.rstudio.com/.

SAS Institute Inc (2018). *SAS© University Edition: Installation Guide for Windows*. Cary, NC: SAS Institute Inc.

SAS Institute Inc (2018). *SAS©OnDemand for Academics: User's Guide*. Cary, NC: SAS Institute Inc.

http://www.sas.com/en_in/company-information/profile.html (accessed April 8, 2019).

https://towardsdatascience.com/ (accessed April 8, 2019).

Weisstein EW. *Hypothesis Testing*. From MathWorld – A Wolfram Web Resource. http://mathworld.wolfram.com/HypothesisTesting.html (accessed April 8, 2019).

SAS for R Users: A Book for Data Scientists, First Edition. Ajay Ohri.
© 2020 John Wiley & Sons, Inc. Published 2020 by John Wiley & Sons, Inc.

Weisstein EW. *Normal Distribution*. From MathWorld – A Wolfram Web Resource. http://mathworld.wolfram.com/NormalDistribution.html (accessed April 8, 2019).

Wickham, H. Tidyverse. Easily Install and Load the 'Tidyverse'. R Package version 1.2.1 https://CRAN.R-project.org/package=tidyverse (accessed April 8, 2019).

Williams, G.J. (2011). *Data Mining with Rattle and R: The Art of Excavating Data for Knowledge Discovery, Use R!* (ed. R. Gentleman, G.G. Parmigiana and K. Hoirnik). New York: Springer.

UCLA: Statistical Consulting Group. *Introduction to SAS*. From https://stats.idre.ucla.edu/sas/output/proc-logistic/ (accessed April 7, 2019).

UCLA: Statistical Consulting Group. Introduction to SAS. From https://stats.idre.ucla.edu/r/dae/logit-regression/ (accessed April 8, 2019).

Index

SAS for R Users: A Book for Data Scientists, First Edition. Ajay Ohri.
© 2020 John Wiley & Sons, Inc. Published 2020 by John Wiley & Sons, Inc.